D.I.Y. RESISTANCE

D.I.Y. RESISTANCE
36 WAYS TO FIGHT BACK!

ANTHONY ALVARADO

Seven Stories Press
New York • Oakland • London

Seven Stories Press
140 Watts Street
New York, NY 10013
www.sevenstories.com

Library of Congress Cataloging-in-Publication Data

Names: Alvarado, Anthony, author.
Title: DIY resistance / Anthony Alvarado.
Other titles: Do it yourself resistance
Description: First Edition. | New York, NY : Seven Stories Press, [2018]
Identifiers: LCCN 2018017398| ISBN 9781609808129 (pbk.) | ISBN 9781609808136 (ebook)
Subjects: LCSH: Government, Resistance to--United States. | Political participation--United States. | Social movements--United States. | Social justice--United States.
Classification: LCC JC328.3 .A45 2018 | DDC 322.40973--dc23
LC record available at https://lccn.loc.gov/2018017398

College professors and middle and high school teachers may order free examination copies of Seven Stories Press titles. To order, visit http://www.sevenstories.com or send a fax on school letterhead to (212) 226-1411.

Book design by Jon Gilbert

Printed in the USA.

9 8 7 6 5 4 3 2 1

CONTENTS

PART 2: FIGHT!

PART 3: LIBERATE!

INTRODUCTION

*What matters is the countless small deeds of unknown people, who lay
the basis for the significant events that enter history.*
—Howard Zinn

ACTION
Choose from the thirty-six actions presented in this
book you can use to fight back against Trump and the
plutocracy and win.

What's the only difference between a wannabe despot and
a real despot?

The courage of those who resist and stand up to him.

We can be one step ahead of him. We know from history
how tyrants operate and how to defeat them—yes! They can
be defeated!

Facing up to tyrants is scary. But we are not alone in walking
this path. We can learn from heroes who have fought this battle
before. We are standing on their shoulders. We have the future
on our side. Remember: more people voted against Donald
Trump than voted for him.

It is an incredibly dangerous time for us as a country; this is easily the biggest challenge we have faced as a nation since the Civil War.

This crisis is an opportunity for courage and for growth.

Historians that study resistance have found no government can ignore the demands of its people when 5 percent of the population engages in collective action. It's called the 5 percent rule. When 5 percent of the people in a country engage in active resistance against an oppressive regime, they bring that authoritarian regime crumbling down, in people-powered nonviolent revolutions—like in Iran in 1979, the Philippines in 1986, and Eastern Europe in 1986.

It is time to take to the streets, to raise our voices, to educate ourselves and to be vigilant and outspoken in our protest.

This book takes its lessons in how to fight back against the Trump presidency from the peaceful warriors, freedom fighters, and courageous leaders in history. We can do more than survive the Trump presidency. So long as we resist we will come through this stronger and better than ever. It is time to fight back.

D.I.Y. Resistance draws inspiration from the American rebel Abbie Hoffman's iconoclastic *Steal This Book*, and it is likewise divided into three parts: "Survive!," "Fight!," and "Liberate!"

In "Survive!," we look at the specifics of how the American democracy is under attack.

In "Resist!," we look at how we can push back against the Trump regime.

In "Liberate!," we look at the path forward, and how to heal this deeply divided nation.

The forces arrayed against us are some of the darkest groups and impulses ever gathered in the history of humanity—Nazis, fascist autocracy, lies, corporate greed, racism.

We fight for equality, and for truth, we fight for fairness.

It is rare for the lines of battle in history to be so sharply delineated, and if ever there was a time to take up the call and join the fray it is now.

The key to defeating the Trump administration is fighting the power of fear with the power of courage. That is what the Resistance needs from you, the reader, your courage. To use the same tools that courageous people like yourself have used throughout history to vanquish the tides of darkness and fear, and to change the world and to make it a better place. It begins with you.

This book is all about the actions we can take to stop the tyrant. Each chapter describes a specific action that you can take. Most you can start doing immediately. I don't expect anyone to be able to do every single one of the actions, myself included. Think of this as a cookbook of recipes. You use a cookbook by trying the recipes you want to try, not by plowing through every single recipe in the exact order in which they are written down. The Resistance is about finding the actions that work for you and doing them. The Resistance is about finding your strength, your voice, your best way of contributing to the fight. Ultimately, like with any movement, we stand together, but it begins with you the individual; therefore the Resistance is a true do-it-yourself movement. Every chapter in this book is centered on an action, something you can DO, not just read about.

High school students in Parkland, Florida, rise up to teach us how to finally win the fight against the guns that have been used to kill kids in school shootings; the teachers of West Virginia rise up and win wage increases not only for themselves but for all public employees in their state; the Time's Up movement creates a new era of equality for women. Each victory makes the next one more likely. Every day, people who were on the sidelines start to enter the fray, finding their courage.

—Anthony Alvarado, March 2018, Portland

PART 1
SURVIVE!

Subcomandante Marcos by Nick D'Auria

1.

FIND YOUR HEROES

*Revolution is not something fixed in ideology, nor is it
something fashioned to a particular decade. It is a
perpetual process embedded in the human spirit.*
—Abbie Hoffman

ACTION

Pick someone who inspires you and hang a picture of
them where you will see it on a daily basis.

RESULT

A daily reminder that people have fought against
oppressive power and made a difference, with grace
and dignity.

Ready to roll up your sleeves and fight back against Trump?
I know it's not going to be easy, and many people are in
despair.

I see people saying, *Screw this. It ain't my problem, I'm going
to just check out and do my own thing for four years.* That is
apathy. Really, it's a form of depression. It's a common reaction.

Another reaction is to go into perpetual panic mode, letting yourself be too overwhelmed to do anything about it.

The most common reaction is probably denial, people saying, *I'm sure it will all work itself out.*

I'm not knocking those emotions. I'm angry and I'm upset about where America's heading, too. It's the five-stages-of-grief thing:

1. Denial
2. Anger
3. Bargaining
4. Depression
5. Acceptance

People are grieving for democracy, and some people's coping strategy is to become stuck in the denial stage and act like it's OK we elected a pathological liar and racist demagogue to office. Apathy is the depression stage. Freaking out is oscillating between the depression and the anger stage. These are natural human reactions to have, but they are debilitating ones. As Einstein said, "The world is a dangerous place to live not because of the people who are evil, but because of the people who don't do anything about it."

Getting stuck in one of the five stages of grief about the Trump presidency and despairing, or bargaining, or just being so upset you can't function, are all different versions of good people not being able to take action. It is time to stop grieving and start resisting: to survive, fight back, and overcome.

There have always been people who've stood up to fascists and demagogues. We need their guidance now more than ever.

Here's the first action of this book: find yourself a hero.

Pick someone inspiring and put their picture up in your room or your office, on your fridge or your bathroom mirror. Somewhere that you are going to see it every day. That's it.

I'm using a picture of Subcomandante Marcos, in fact it's the same portrait that's included in this book. If you want you can just tear out (or photocopy) one of the many hero portraits from the book you hold in your hands right now!

I know some people might have a hard time doing this, it is completely earnest, and it is easier to be cynical than sincere. Cynicism is really just a defense mechanism, a way of avoiding the hard work that demands doing. It is not time for cynicism; it is time for hope, and it is time to fight in earnest.

Our heroes show us that against all odds, in the face of great challenges, the human spirit can overcome oppression and fear. This is a deep truth. Even the tales we grew up on and tell our children are stories of courage and action in the face of oppression: think of Luke Skywalker answering the call to join the rebels, Harry Potter growing up to defeat Voldemort, Frodo Baggins battling against the Dark Lord, Katniss Everdeen leading the fight against the plutocracy of President Snow. These are stories of resistance against great odds. Heroic rebellion against evil rulers is deep within the DNA of humanity.

Some Heroes to Get You Started

Martin Luther King Jr.: African American civil rights leader; led nonviolent resistance, marches, and boycotts; gave speeches; fought against segregation and won.

"Our lives begin to end the day we become silent about things that matter."

Mahatma Gandhi: Leader of the protests that freed India from the British Empire. Also worked to expand women's rights, end the oppression of the poor, and expand peace to all religions in his country.

"Power based on love is a thousand times more effective and permanent than the one derived from fear of punishment."

Harriet Tubman: A leader of the Underground Railroad, she guided escaped slaves from the South to safety in the North. A radical, working in secrecy, and risking her safety for what she believed in.

"I had reasoned this out in my mind, there was one of two things I had the right to, liberty or death: if I could not have one I would have the other."

Subcomandante Marcos: Masked rebel leader of the Zapatista army, a warrior and writer who used radical tactics to raise awareness of the plight of poor indigenous Mayan people in Chiapas, Mexico, in their struggle for social rights.

"We are nothing if we walk alone; we are everything when we walk together in step with other dignified feet."

Abbie Hoffman: Radical and protestor who used theatrical techniques like levitating the Pentagon with psychic energy to raise awareness of the Vietnam War.

"The only way to support a revolution is to make your own."

Nina Simone: Incredible musician and powerful singer who used her voice to sing songs of protest against racism.

"There's no excuse for the young people not knowing who the heroes and heroines are or were."

Cesar Chavez: Leader of Mexican American rights, activist for farmers. Fought for higher wages for immigrants, known for using nonviolent but aggressive tactics, also used fasting as a tool to raise awareness.

"Preservation of one's culture does not require contempt or disrespect for other cultures."

Alicia Garza: Not every activist hero is found in history books, people are fighting for what they believe right now. Consider Garza, cofounder of the Black Lives Matter movement. What began as a series of tweets in response to systemic police shootings of African Americans has grown into a huge activist movement. Garza is an example of a modern-day activist with an awareness of how social media can be a powerful tool for change, but also an awareness that stopping at Internet activism is not enough.

"What it takes to get people from liking and sharing and retweeting to organizing is a hard and long process."

Aaron Swartz: A teenage computer prodigy and super-geek who helped design Reddit, Creative Commons, RSS, and other programs, who fought against Internet censorship and for keeping the Internet free of corporate control. He was vindictively hounded by the US government for downloading academic journals from MIT, because they wanted to set an example of him as an Internet hacktivist. Swartz was threatened with imprisonment and fines until eventually he took his own life.

"There is no justice in following unjust laws."

Jasilyn Charger: She is not famous, or even very well known. She is an example of the truth that you don't have to be a famous person with a million Twitter followers to make a dent in the world, and to plant the seeds that cause change. Charger and her friends, a group of teenagers who gathered as a prayer group, were among the first five people to camp at Standing Rock in protest, to raise awareness of the Dakota Access Pipeline—an oil pipeline threatening local water on Native American land. This small group grew to become a camp of thousands, raising awareness on a national level of the struggle of the people to protect what they hold sacred from corporate greed and pollution.

"There is a prophecy from the time of Sitting Bull. That in seven generations from then, the youth will rise up. That they will be awakened."

These are just a few examples of the heroes of the ongoing revolution that is in progress.

Freedom has never been given freely; it has always been fought for, as we must fight for it now.

Welcome to the Resistance.

Harriet Tubman by Elizabeth Haidle

2.
SEE THE BIG PICTURE

We are a country that has far more problems than it deserves and far more solutions than it applies. This is due heavily to the control of the many by the few, which creates a democracy gap filled by a plutocracy.
—Ralph Nader

ACTION
Look at the big picture to understand the forces at work behind the headlines.

RESULT
See beyond the distractions to understand the con game of the plutocracy and the need for progressive policies that fight back!

We must not let ourselves become so distracted by Trump's reality-show buffoonery that we lose track of the real-life damage being done by the legislation passed under this administration. It is important to understand the big picture—the problem we are up against is not just Donald Trump, he is the figurehead for a deeper and older rot. The policy and legislation being rammed through, that is so harmful to everyday

Americans on so many issues, has one thing in common. It is beneficial to the rich. We can fight back by championing policy that is by the people and for the people.

The plutocracy—people like the Koch brothers—use the power of their money to shape politics so that they can make even more obscene amounts of money.

The plutocrats pay off the politicians through campaign contributions. They also have huge amounts of money and control in right-wing media, such as Rupert Murdoch's Fox News. They use henchmen—politicians like Paul Ryan, thousands of behind-the-scenes lobbyists, and right-wing pundits like Sean Hannity—to shape public opinion. With their vast wealth, they are buying two things: the legislative policy they want (deregulating business so they can make even more money and keep it for themselves and their dynasties) and a media machine to bamboozle the right-wing base into thinking this is somehow in their best interest. They are using obscene wealth to increase their obscene wealth. The harmful policies being passed by the Republican Congress only make sense when this big picture is understood.

To sum it up, the con game works like this:

1. The plutocracy has an unequal share of the nation's wealth so . . .
2. they fund politicians, who in turn . . .
3. legislate deregulations and tax cuts that funnel money back to the plutocracy.

Rinse. Repeat. And the cycle continues. We have to break this corrosive cycle that is designed to funnel wealth to the top of the pyramid.

The Plutocracy

While Trump soaks up everybody's attention span and the headlines, the plutocracy is robbing the country blind. America's plutocrats are using the Trump era to roll back regulations and industry safeguards so that the already wealthy can get themselves an even larger slice of the pie, at the expense of the poor and middle class. In order to grab themselves more money, they lowered taxes on corporations, ended net neutrality, attacked affordable health care, stole protected natural wildlife lands, and that's just the beginning. Left unchecked, they will only use their increased power and wealth to buy, swindle, and steal more power and wealth for themselves. They are attempting to warp our democracy into a system where they have all the power and the bought-and-paid politicians do their bidding. While wages for the lower and middle classes have stagnated for the past three decades, the richest 1 percent have seen their incomes spike by 275 percent.

While it can seem like a lot to keep track of, the motives of the kleptocracy are easy to understand. Money. Greed. Self-interest. That's it in a nutshell. This is not really anything new, it is in fact about as old as money itself. Remember the 1920s? No, of course not, unless you happen to be a hundred years old. But we know from history, books, and movies what that was like. The wealth built up during the Gilded Age fueled the extravagant luxury seen on shows like *Downton Abbey*. In case you never watched the show, it involves a rich family who is served by a caste of lower-class servants who do the dishes, the cooking, the chores, and help the lord and lady of the manor to dress themselves.

While the upper crust isn't currently going about in monocles and bustles, the economics are all too familiar. The richest 1 percent own more than half the world's wealth. In the U.S. in the past four decades the richest 1 percent have accounted for 39 percent of America's wealth. The four hundred richest people in America now control more wealth than the bottom 50 percent of people in America. This is not by accident. It is a byproduct of the deregulation of the finance market. The rich make money by moving money around. Meanwhile the working class is squeezed out as more jobs are moved offshore. This imbalance is staggering, and it is that way by design—it will only get worse until people rise up and protest and organize and fight back. The rich are consciously, actively using wealth to rig the system in their favor. Money is behind all of the politics.

There can be no *Downton Abbey* without the other side of the coin—*The Grapes of Wrath*. In the city where I live, the streets and neighborhoods are filling up more and more with homeless people who can't afford basic shelter and so live in piles of blankets under doorways, and in cars, tents, and shantytowns.

Forty-one million Americans (more than the combined populations of Texas, Michigan, and Maine) are living in poverty today. It doesn't matter to them if the stock market is doing well; these forty-one million Americans can't benefit from investments when they can't afford dinner.

While this tragedy is going on, we live in a nation that just gave the largest tax break ever to corporations and the wealthy! The tax scam passed by the Republican-controlled Congress in the dead of night was a $1.3 trillion transfer of wealth from the middle and working classes to the wealthiest tranche of Americans. Ladies and gentlemen, it does not make sense and it is morally wrong. Understand that the greed of the super rich has a real and human price. The greed of the billionaires is paid for in full at the cost of the homeless, at the cost of drilling for oil in the oceans and selling millions of acres of public land—these are the bargains with the devil that must be made for such obscene amounts of wealth to be concentrated into the hands of so few.

The Henchmen

Trump's cabinet is one of the wealthiest gangs of rich fat cats ever assembled, and also the most white and male of any presidential cabinet since Ronald Reagan's. These henchmen are more than willing to steal from the poor and to pollute the air we breathe and the water we drink in order to make money. These people are heartless in their pursuit of wealth. These are people who will use any dirty trick they can, including harnessing racism in the name of nationalism, but ultimately it is all in the name of heartbreaking financial greed.

In case after case, the person Trump picked as chair of each federal department is there to roll back regulations and dismantle the protections that the department is meant to provide the American people. From education and the EPA to housing and the FCC, the people in Trump's cabinet are the definition of "the fox guarding the henhouse." Here are a few prime examples.

Ben Pruitt: Trump's Environmental Protection Agency chief thinks modern air is too clean. (WTF?!) He brought with him a host of "scientists" from the oil and chemical industries. It is like putting Ronald McDonald in charge of the Food and Drug Administration. Pruitt's main goal is less regulation. Starting to sound familiar?

Betsy DeVos: Secretary of Education DeVos wants to privatize the public education system—in other words, run our nation's education system as just another sector of business that the rich can profit from instead of being provided equally to all.

Ajit Pai: Trump's FCC chairman Ajit Pai, a former Verizon lawyer, abolished the net neutrality laws that protected the Internet from censorship and made it so that providers could not charge different people different amounts to access the

Internet. Another case of a person whose main interest is attacking consumer protection regulations in order to help out big business. He has raised caps on how much broadband providers can charge customers while cutting back on a program for low-income broadband Internet. What a guy.

Steve Mnuchin: Treasury Secretary Mnuchin, poster boy for the new Gilded Age, is the über-wealthy Goldman Sachs banker Trump placed at the helm of the national treasury. Super rich and entitled, to the point that he used government planes for personal trips to the tune of $800,000 of taxpayer money. That's almost a million tax dollars spent just on private plane rides. Of course, a million dollars is not much to this plutocrat. Mnuchin had $100 million in offshore accounts that he "failed to report." He is an expert in using offshore tax havens to hide his money. He made his fortune by being overly aggressive in foreclosing on people's homes. Since he built his fortune taking advantage of poorer people, it seems his current position is a natural extension.

Legislation for the Rich by the Rich

Understanding that the legislation being passed is designed to help funnel more money and power to the wealthiest individuals in America is the only way to make sense of the Trump administration.

- Trump's huge tax cuts for the rich: the bill gives 83 percent of its tax cuts to guess who . . . the 1 percent wealthiest. The Paul Ryan–engineered, lobbyist-approved scam cuts taxes on everyone in the short term but only benefits the wealthy and corporations in the long term.
- To pay for the tax cuts, Republicans will make cuts to Medicare, Social Security, and benefits for the poor.
- With the repeal of net neutrality, Internet providers can charge different amounts for different packages. Net neutrality mandated that all ISPs display all websites at the same speed to all sources of Internet traffic. Now ISPs will be free to sell different "bundles" so that a basic package that can access only a few websites while a "premium" package could cost much more.
- The repeal of the individual insurance mandate. This will raise premiums and lower health care enrollment, a move designed to weaken affordable health care.
- Slashing millions of acres of national protected wildlands. Reducing the size of the Bears Ears monument by 85 percent and slashing the Grand Staircase in half, reducing these national monuments by two million acres. Setting a precedent to slash other protected wildlands.

- Rolling back a host of regulations in less publicized areas. Keep in mind that many of the deregulations happening under the Trump administration are in areas that don't receive much attention from the headline news. For this reason, they are being snuck through—safeguards and regulations are being reversed and stripped without many people even being aware of this. For example, the EPA approving harmful chlorpyrifos, an insecticide used on crops that poisons the water of rural communities, despite the recommendation of EPA scientists to ban the toxins. Another example: passing laws that make it so the elderly cannot sue if they are abused in nursing homes. And scheming to weaken and dismantle the Consumer Protection Bureau, which works to protect the public from predatory loan schemes like payday loans.
- Ordering to advance the construction of the Keystone XL and Dakota Access oil pipelines, despite the protest of the Standing Rock Sioux Tribe.
- Reversing the Waters of United States rule, which protected wetlands and headwaters from being damaged by developers. Trump described these habitats as "puddles" during his signing of this legislation.
- Putting an end to a bill protecting our nation's lakes and rivers from coal waste.

- The EPA has adopted a policy of ignoring polluters so that smokestacks, waste pipelines, trash incinerators, and so on can pump pollution into the air, the soil, and the waters of America, and polluters know that the federal government will wink and look the other way.

Here is one more example: the chemical perfluorooctanoic acid causes cancer and birth defects. For years, the EPA has worked to prevent its use in products because it's very, very bad for humans. But under Trump's administration, a top EPA deputy hastily rewrote the regulations, making it harder to track this poison. This is a despicable but typical example. It is not even a well-known issue; after all, who can remember the word perfluorooctanoic acid—and it is difficult to keep track of things like this when Trump is grabbing the headlines each day by doing things like threatening to wipe North Korea off the face of the planet, or destroy the rule of law by firing anybody investigating him. And yet people will die because of this, and people will be born disfigured because of this. Why? So that some corporation can make more money.

Immoral things are being done while the public is distracted by Trump's circus barker performance. It reminds me of a shoplifting scheme some small-time grifters used to run at a bookstore I worked at during college. They would run the scam in pairs. A couple would come in, and one of them would throw a big commotion, they would shout, get into a fight with an innocent bystander, swear, rant and rave and act like a raging toddler. All the bookstore employees focused on dealing with the person throwing an aggressive tantrum, and we would work to kick that person out of the bookstore. Only afterward did we realize that while we were so focused on the loudmouth, the sneaky, much quieter partner was shoplifting like crazy—stuffing the most expensive textbooks they could grab into a duffel bag for as long as the distraction went on. Then the two shoplifters would go across town to sell the textbooks and split the profits. It's a classic two-bit scam. Trump is the distraction. The plutocracy is the other half of the shoplifting team. It is the same scam but for trillions of dollars.

Legislation by the People for the People

These are human-caused problems and they have solutions; they are not impossible to fix—but we have to recognize what we are up against in order to overcome their selfish con game.

Here are some great examples of positive legislative actions we can push for to shift the balance of power back to the people. These are the kinds of changes we can make if America is ruled by the people, not the plutocrats.

The backlash is surely coming, and we should use it to create a democracy for the people, not just the rich.

RAISE TAXES ON THE RICH

Until the day that there are not thousands of homeless Americans, it is wrong for one out of a thousand Americans to accrue obscene amounts of wealth that they cannot even spend in one lifetime. Taxes on those who make more than $500,000 a year should be raised to 75 percent. This would be similar to the most progressive tax rates in US history, during 1944, when a 94 percent tax rate applied to incomes above $200,000. The tax rate remained high during the '50s, '60s, and '70s, never dipping below 70 percent for the wealthiest individuals, and those were decades of prosperity for the entire country, not just the wealthy elite.

SINGLE-PAYER HEALTH CARE

With single-payer health care, *everybody* has their health care covered. Right now fifty million Americans can't afford health care. Having all health care provided by one system streamlines everything—which allows for massive savings of over $350 billion annually. We spend twice as much per person on health care as any other nation. Single-payer would fix that. A single-payer system already exists in America; it's called Medicare, which is health care for Americans over sixty-five. A simple way to enact single-payer health care would be to expand the Medicare age down from sixty-five to cover everyone. We are the only wealthy industrialized modern society that lacks universal health care!

RAISE THE MINIMUM WAGE TO $15 AN HOUR

Far too many people are living in poverty in America. The federal minimum wage of $7.25 is hopelessly out of date. No one can afford to pay for a place to live and food to eat on seven bucks an hour. A better minimum wage is overdue.

HOLD WALL STREET ACCOUNTABLE: REINSTATE GLASS-STEAGALL

Regulations protect us from the greed of Wall Street bankers. Recent history has shown this is a very necessary safeguard! Glass-Steagall separates commercial banks, which are federally guaranteed, from investment banks. We should reinstate this common-sense legislation that prevented banks from gambling with depositors' money. It prevents banks from taking on high risk—its repeal directly led to the risky business that caused the Great Recession. Without it, wealthy bankers can take on risky investments and then be bailed out by taxpayers when it goes wrong.

CLEAN ENERGY

Imagine a nation where energy is 100 percent renewable. Through a combination of wind, water, and solar energy, it is possible. It's a matter of working toward a future that benefits the earth and generations to come, instead of just a future that benefits the bottom line of oil companies. Mandating 100 percent clean, renewable energy would take a lot of work; in fact, that is a good thing, because it would also create millions of jobs. More importantly the planet would not be doomed to overheating and mass extinctions just so a few billionaires can buy themselves yachts and fancy watches.

BAN OFFSHORE DRILLING

Should nature, wildlife, and people suffer for the sake of the profit of oil companies? When the Exxon Valdez leak of 2010 happened (On Rex Tillerson's watch), thousands of miles of ocean were contaminated in the Gulf of Mexico, killing untold numbers of fish and wildlife and causing health problems for residents of the gulf area that persist to this day. We should demand that Congress protect our oceans. The Trump administration is currently trying to reverse an Obama-era ban on offshore drilling in 120 million acres of ocean waters.

PROTECT PUBLIC LANDS

A corporation would sell any and everything to make a buck. If they could, they would sell off the air we breathe, and the mountains, the moon, and the rivers. That is why we need laws that don't let them destroy the environment, laws that protect the natural beauty of this country and the national monuments from being sold off to the rich.

MAKE COLLEGE FREE

Germany, the Czech Republic, Sweden, Denmark, Norway, and France all offer free college education to their residents. There is no reason America could not choose to invest in future generations rather than saddling them with crippling life-long debt.

GUN CONTROL

Mass shootings (defined as an event where at least four people are shot) happen every day in America. Sadly, there is a real danger of people becoming anesthetized to this unnecessary violence. On average thirty people are killed a day by guns in America. There is constantly a fresh horrible tragedy in the news where scores of people are gunned down, and each time the politicians claim "now is not the time to politicize this tragedy." Nowhere is safe, children are shot in schools, people are murdered in churches, at concerts, at dance clubs. twenty first graders were shot at Sandy Hook. And each time tragedy such as this unfolds we are told there is nothing that can be done. That is a lie told because guns are a multibillion-dollar industry. Gun control works. When gun control was enacted in Australia the occurrence of mass shootings dropped to zero and gun-related homicides dropped by 59 percent. We can start with a common-sense ban on things like assault rifles, and by closing the "private sale loopholes" that allow people to buy guns without undergoing any sort of background check. These measures would go a long way toward preventing the next Sandy Hook, the next Orlando, the next Las Vegas.

BRING BACK NET NEUTRALITY

Net neutrality means Internet providers treat all websites the same. Without it, an Internet provider can slow access for certain sites, or charge more to access some websites. We should reinstate net neutrality, and this time make it a federal bill so it can't be revoked by a panel of three Republican votes.

REVERSE *CITIZENS UNITED*: A CORPORATION IS NOT A PERSON

The *Citizens United* ruling of 2010 gave corporations a green light to spend unlimited amounts on ads in political campaigns. Corporations have spent billions since then influencing political campaigns, and look at where it has gotten us. This unlimited corporate spending was allowed because the Supreme Court said that this was free speech for the corporations. The four dissenting judges stated the obvious: a corporation is not a person, and it does not deserve the same protections to free speech that a person has under the Constitution. This terrible Supreme Court decision (thanks a lot, Scalia) is a big part of why we are in the mess we're in now. We need to demand that our elected officials pass new, stronger legislation, undoing the damage done by the *Citizens United* ruling.

A corporation is not a person. A corporation is a greedy force designed to make money. Corporate greed does not care about you or your children; for a profit it will give you cancer, for a profit it will give you diabetes and high cholesterol. For a profit it will trap you in debt, or sell you a bogus degree from a fraudulent university. For a profit it will always give you the worst deal it can afford to give you. For a profit it will stifle creativity, for a profit it will poison the seas and the rivers, kill all the fish, and charge you more per month not to censor your Internet. All corporations are essentially the same thing, a greedy brute blind force, designed to do one thing only: make more profit.

We Can Do Better!

If we organize, we can wrest control from the rich and give the power back to the people. They did it in the '60s, with the mass demonstrations by the young people, and marches for women's rights and black civil rights. Until we wake up and fight back with as much organization and feet in the street as was seen in the '60s, the plutocracy will continue to use their power and money and henchmen to warp politics and give themselves more power and money in the vicious cycle that is the current big picture.

What we want is not radical, although we are told by the establishment that these ideas are too far-out and cannot be done. That is a lie. What we want is the will of the people. The more people understand the benefits of common-sense, good policies like universal health care, reasonable gun control, and making college available to all, the more likely we are to get there—don't let anyone tell you we must give up on a good and beneficial idea because it is "not practical."

It is common sense that we should end senseless gun violence in this country, it is common sense that not all of the money should be concentrated in the hands of so few, it is common sense that in a country as rich as ours we should not have forty-one million people living in poverty.

The status quo is in fact radical in its obscenity, the plutocracy is radical in its concentration of wealth and power into the hands of the few. It is time for the rest of America to rise up and say enough!

3.

PLUG INTO YOUR COMMUNITY

People who give you their food give you their heart.
—Cesar Chavez

ACTION

Plug into your local resistance community.

RESULT

Make it real by engaging in real-life resistance.

Picture the many leaves and branches of a giant oak tree. The larger branches split into smaller branches, which split yet again, smaller and smaller, branching out into green leaves. Each individual leaf has its own place on the tree, and they all work together to grow. The Resistance is like a huge tree of many leaves, branches, and roots.

In order for the tree of the Resistance to grow, we must connect with our friends, families, communities, and networks and talk about what is happening. The branches of this tree are the many vital causes that we must fight for: the branch to fight racism, the branch to guard freedom of religion, the branch to

Martin Luther King Jr. by Amy Kuttab

protect the environment, and so on, these are all a part of the same thing—the Resistance. We are all part of the same tree, united and on the same side. Resistance begins with community.

Find strength in your community. Your community is your leaf, and that is where you have the greatest impact. It is the people you see and talk to every week, it is the friends that you hang out with, it is your family, it is your church, it is book clubs and pick-up basketball games and BBQs. It is people being together and spending time together. It is our communities that will decide the future. Be vocal in your

> It is important that you don't try
> to fight tyranny all alone.

community that you oppose Trump. When despots become widely unpopular enough, even their own party will turn against them.

Seek out like-minded people in your community. They are the building blocks of what you and every other person who stands against Trump are: the Resistance. It is from the strength of each other, the human connections of those who stand with us, that we build strength.

Identify who your allies are. We must band together to become a voice too loud to be silenced. The strength of the

mightiest oak comes from the combined work of all the roots
and leaves.

4.
KNOW YOUR ENEMY

The farther back you can look, the farther
forward you are likely to see.
—Winston Churchill

ACTION
Take Trump's threats seriously. Believe that he intends
to do what he has said. Understand what he is by
comparing him to other despots in history.

RESULT
A clear-eyed understanding of the psychology of
President Trump and villains like him.

While Trump, with his gaudy lies and disdain for facts, is a uniquely American demagogue, he is bred from the same strain as every other demagogue. Here is the basic recipe for every demagogue: a bottomless hunger to further his own power, uncanny knowledge of how to manipulate his followers, media savvy, and a lack of human empathy. Tony Schwartz, Trump's ghostwriter for his autobiography *The Art of the Deal*, called Trump a sociopath. The mark of a sociopath is a fluid mastery of lying. Tony Schwartz described Trump by saying "he's a living black hole!" A black hole using empty promises to lure victims reminds me of the creature No-Face from Miyazaki's anime masterpiece *Spirited Away*. No-Face is a hungry ghost who offers people whatever they want, but when they approach him he swallows them up and they become part of the monster.

Trump always has plenty of praise for the "leadership" of bloody dictators, despots, and demagogues. He has praised war criminals like Vladimir Putin, Recep Erdoğan, Bashar al-Assad, Muammar Gaddafi, Saddam Hussein. If Hitler were alive today, Trump would no doubt praise his "strong leadership style." These are the kinds of people Trump looks up to and admires. These are dictators who have slaughtered their own people by the thousands. They are his role models.

The psychology of this sort of ruler is called fascism. We humans are not always rational creatures, and because of this we can fall prey to making irrational, fear-driven decisions. Fascism happens when demagogues take power by fear. A demagogue is one who knows how to stoke those fears in crowds, and then promises they alone can assuage them. It's been done a thousand times throughout history. Spoiler alert: the results are not pretty.

Fascism is a far-right movement led by a dictator; it is democracy's only natural predator. Here is a list of the fourteen characteristics of fascist leadership, according to political scientist Dr. Lawrence Britt, who looked at the common traits of Hitler, Mussolini, Franco, Suharto, and Pinochet. This list was written in 2003, well before there was even a glimmer of the Trump presidency on the horizon

(Trump was busy stiffing the people he hired to design his golf club-house.) Check off the traits that match Trump.

The Fourteen Characteristics of Fascism:

1. Powerful and Continuing Nationalism
2. Disdain for the Recognition of Human Rights
3. Identification of Enemies/Scapegoats as a Unifying Cause
4. Supremacy of the Military
5. Rampant Sexism
6. Controlled Mass Media
7. Obsession with National Security
8. Religion and Government Are Intertwined
9. Corporate Power Is Protected
10. Labor Power Is Suppressed
11. Disdain for Intellectuals and the Arts
12. Obsession with Crime and Punishment
13. Rampant Cronyism and Corruption
14. Fraudulent Elections

That was a pretty easy pop quiz, wasn't it? Nationalism, check, disdain for human rights, check, scapegoating, sexism, check, check. Trump clearly meets the criteria of a fascist. He is not really a Republican, but something else entirely, a parasite that hijacked the Republican Party. Understanding how fascist dictators operate is the first step to understanding how to defeat one. Consider one of the only people Trump has consistently praised, besides himself.

Vladimir Putin is as dangerous, cold-hearted, and cunning as a shark. He honed his style of covert and unscrupulous power by rising through the ranks of the KGB. Putin is as at home in the world of organized crime as he is in global politics. His long-term goal is to make Russia a superpower again by undermining Western democracy, which he sees as a natural and historic enemy to his Russian oligarchy. Putin wants our democracy to fail. He has been in power in one form or another for over twenty-six years, and he is playing a long-term game. For Putin, helping to get Trump elected was just one move in an ongoing game of global chess. Putin is shrewd and sneaky, the tactics he used to influence the 2016 US election (by directing Russian hackers to hack the DNC and release stolen information to WikiLeaks, and by flooding Facebook, Twitter, and the Internet with fake news via Russian bots and blogs) are the same tricks of subterfuge and disinformation he has used in other places, like the Ukraine, and that he will continue to use in Europe and in future American elections. He is openly admired by Trump. Putin is ruthless. To Putin there is no line between military warfare and warfare by propaganda, blackmail, lies, and intimidation. He is rumored to secretly be the richest man in the world. Outspoken Russian critics of Putin have been beaten, poisoned, shot, pushed out of windows, and imprisoned.

The fascist worldview is that it's the nation versus everybody else, and all the problems of the nation are blamed on a scapegoat, some minority group. It's easier to blame somebody else than to come up with real solutions. It is essentially an ideology about being "strong" by being a bully. Researchers who study human psychology have determined that a certain percentage of people have an authoritarian personality type. They are drawn to strongman leadership. This personality type likes rules and rulers; it is basically a reaction to fear, to feeling afraid, and a lack of control in

....

The better job we do as the Resistance, the more
we can lessen the damage of this monster.

....

the world. It is a mindset that says—"I'm scared, I want a strong leader to take control, to tell me what to do, so I don't have to worry." It is the opposite of a mindset of courage and feeling like you as an individual can take care of yourself. It is a remnant from tribal days, when humans lived in small groups that would often fight each other. When people feel afraid, scared, threatened, there is a part of human nature that looks for an authoritarian leader to take control. That basic human psychology is still with us; when it operates on the large scale of a nation, it leads to fascism.

People are more willing to give up their freedom when they are fearful. Fear works the same way whether there is really something to be afraid of or not. The demagogue understands this and creates a bogeyman out of a minority group that the demagogue can "save" his followers from. For Trump it is Muslims and Mexicans, and for Hitler it was the Jews.

In times of perceived crisis, some people are willing to hand over the reins of free thought and let someone else take power and make all the decisions. The stronger the group mentality is, the more people shut down their rational thinking. Trump appeals directly to people's basest emotions: fear, racism, and the instinctual need to feel a part of a group.

Trump skips past all reason and works directly on the animal brain, the instincts of the group mentality, using racism and xenophobia to make people feel afraid, and then to promise them that he can "make everything better." The inevitable strategy of the tyrant is to get people scared enough that they are willing to trade freedom for a false sense of security. For this reason dangers are played up, exaggerated, and even faked. For Hitler this was the Reichstag fire, which he used as an excuse to jail and silence his opponents.

Some may think comparing Trump to Hitler, to Putin, to Pinochet, is alarmist, but to take that stance is to ignore all of the authoritarian actions Trump has already carried out. During his first year, President Trump's first presidential decree was the unconstitutional Muslim ban—barring travelers from Iran, Syria, Libya, Somalia, Yemen, and Chad. He also ruthlessly cut off the DACA program, marking eight hundred thousand young Dreamers who were brought to the US as children for deportation. His justification for attacking immigrants is grounded in racism; he has compared refugees to "vomit" and ranted about immigrants to his cabinet, saying Haitian immigrants "all have AIDS" and Nigerians visiting America would never "go back to their huts." Meanwhile Attorney General Jeff Sessions has worked to make the justice system more draconian, stripping federal prosecutors of their discretion to decide what punishment fits the crime and instead mandating the maximum sentences for all cases. The Center for Disease Control issued a list of banned words—barring the use of "fetus," "science-based," "transgender," "vulnerable," "entitlement," and "diversity." The EPA has worked to purge references to climate change. The Department of Justice also halted a program created after the police brutality of Ferguson, and police departments across the country are once again being allowed to stockpile military weapons—bayonets, grenade launchers, unmanned aerial vehicles, camouflaged armor and armored vehicles—for use against civilians. The military and the CIA have also eliminated measures designed to protect civilians from drone strikes.

While the government under Trump has become more authoritarian and xenophobic in word and deed, it has simultaneously become much more corrupt and opaque. The first bill Trump signed was to rescind the Dodd-Frank anti-corruption rule, so that oil and mining companies no longer have to disclose payments to foreign governments. Meanwhile the labor department is no longer enforcing overtime payment for employees, and will no longer fight against pay discrimination by age, race, or gender. The FCC abolished net neutrality, ignoring the demands of the American constituents in favor of the demands of big business. Government agencies across the board have changed their websites to share less information with the public. Similarly, one of the first changes in White House policy was to stop keeping logs of White House visitors—hiding who has direct access to the president. Perhaps most frightening of all, the Republican establishment has happily gone along with Trump, turning a blind eye to his authoritarian overreach and mounting evidence of collusion with Russia in order to pass their tax cuts for the rich.

There is plenty to be alarmed about. The warning signs are blatant. There were plenty of people who thought that being afraid of the Third Reich was alarmist at the time, and it was only after World War II ended that the full extent of the Holocaust was understood.

Hitler also rose to power legally. He was elected after he had made a name for himself speaking to packed audiences, and promising to make Germany great again. The message is hauntingly familiar: that the nation must rise to greatness "again," and the obstacle to that is racial minorities. This call to "make America great again" is a promise to go back to whiter, more racist times, when it was socially acceptable to be racist, to treat blacks, and women, and Hispanics, and Asians, as second-class citizens.

Authoritarian leaders, by nature, always press to increase their hold on power. The political story of Hitler illustrates this psychology of creeping authoritarianism in action. Adolf Hitler was elected to chancellor (the equivalent of our presidency) in 1933. He then fought to achieve full control over Germany's legislative and executive branches of government. He claimed he would use democratic elections, but soon he was using blackmail against his opponents, jailing his enemies, and intimidating all who opposed him, until they had either given up or been hauled away to concentration camps. Fascists fight as dirty as they can. Once they have won more power, they use it to fight dirtier.

Hitler was still treated as just a regular politician until it was too late. The Holocaust killed eleven million people. The Nazis slaughtered Jews, Soviet prisoners, Polish people, as well as homosexuals, the disabled, Roma, Jehovah's Witnesses, and trade unionists. But even Hitler didn't start out by openly proposing the Holocaust, he started by saying he would make Germany great again, and by scapegoating minorities for the nation's problems.

During his rise to power Hitler was not taken seriously, he was seen by many Germans as a buffoon. When Hitler made the Jewish people wear yellow stars for identification (they didn't have computer databases back then), most people thought that it would just end there. As he ramped up the racism that lead to the Holocaust, people thought, "oh, it's just words" and "this can't be happening, no need to be alarmist." The hugeness of the evil that he unleashed was so large, many people at the time were not able to see it coming.

We should take the things Trump says seriously. He is writing his dark motives into action and legislation on a daily basis. He has said he would like to bomb the shit out of the Middle East. He has said he would like to jail his opponents. He has said he would bring back torture. He has said he will deport millions and build a wall. He has said that he would shut down mosques, force all American Muslims to register in a national database, and put Muslims in camps.

In the first months of his presidency Trump resolved to end the DACA program, thereby threatening eight hundred thousand children with deportation from the country where they have grown up. These are real kids, children who came to America before their sixteenth birthday, many as infants—real lives, real families will be hurt by this. He vocally came out in support of neo-Nazis and white nationalists, equating them with activists, after the white supremacists rampaged in Charlottesville, Virginia, with swastikas, Confederate flags, and violence fueled by racial hatred. He has continued to deny climate change and backed out of the Paris climate accord, even as the forests of the West Coast burned and the people of Texas and Florida had their homes destroyed by hurricanes and floods.

While the psychology of power-hungry autocrats is always the same, the outcome is shaped by what holds them in check— and depends on whether society pushes back and speaks out against their power, or not.

America has good things going for it in the struggle to survive the Trump presidency: we have the Constitution, the judicial system, freedom of the press, and free speech. The will of the majority opposes him. Resistance is the balancing force against the tyranny of evil men.

5.
TAKE CARE OF
YOURSELF

It is better to light one small candle than to curse the darkness.
—Confucius

ACTION
Commit to doing something that recharges your own
personal battery on (at least) a weekly basis.

RESULT
The energy and optimism needed to be effective.

I worked for years as a social worker in mental health, with mentally ill and homeless people. It was a tough job that took a lot out of people's batteries emotionally. Time and time again, I'd see new social workers burn out and quit because they didn't take the time to step back from the work and take care of themselves emotionally and physically. The paradox was that often the people who threw themselves into the work the hardest were the same ones who burned out. They were so focused on trying to take care of others, they forgot that first you need to take care of yourself.

The best way to combat emotional burnout is to not let yourself even get there in the first place. Which is why you must keep your inner battery fully charged. That means taking time out to focus on other stuff. With so much at stake, it is easy to think your own emotional health is not a factor, but nothing could be further from the truth. Think of yourself as a soldier in a battle, or an athlete who is preparing for the competition of their lifetime. You want to be in the best shape you can be in. That means taking good care of yourself. Guard against fatigue.

··

You refuel the gas in your car before you hit empty.
Do at least as much for yourself.

··

Pick something that keeps you healthy and grounded, and commit to doing it on a regular basis. Remind yourself that doing this recharging activity is an essential piece of doing your part.

The best activity to choose will be different for everyone. I go jogging. It's a simple, easy-to-do activity that keeps my emotions and energy balanced and positive. Do whatever it is that makes you feel happy and relaxed. Pick something and commit to doing it regularly.

Maybe the activity that recharges you is physical, or maybe it is creative, or maybe it's just relaxing. It doesn't matter what it is: cooking, yoga, fly-fishing, or whatever. What matters is that you commit to recharging your batteries. Take a hike, go to the movies, I dunno, go hot-air ballooning, whatever it is that you do to relax. Do it often, and do it fully. The important thing is that you connect to yourself through this weekly action, this recharge time for yourself. This action is just as important as everything else in this book. Pick one thing and do it at least once a week.

Some ideas:
Go for a hike
Read a good book
Cook a homemade meal
Take a nap
Do some gardening
Take a yoga class
Go dancing
Go for a bike ride
Give someone a hug
Spend an afternoon all by yourself
Spend an afternoon hanging out with a friend
Walk the dog
You get the idea

Noam Chomsky by Amy Kuttab

6.

READ INSPIRING BOOKS

*If we are to change our world view, images have to change. The artist
now has a very important job to do. He's not a little peripheral figure
entertaining rich people, he's really needed.*
—Vaclav Havel

ACTION
Be inspired by some of the smartest ideas and voices
that have ever stood against authoritarianism.

RESULT
Books not only inspire, they can show the
path of best Resistance.

Reading inspiring books provides mental fuel, energy, and ideas for our actions. A book is the best way I know for finding information, strategies, ideas—if it is true that knowledge is power, then books are weapons. Make no mistake, this is a battle, arm yourself! There is a reason why oppressive regimes have long sought to ban books that criticize tyranny, despotism, and demagoguery.

Books are inherently radical. (In the modern Internet age,

they are more radical than ever.) I see them as a natural antidote to the shallow information overload that we constantly swim through these days, thanks to the Internet. Reading a book forces us to slow down. Your mind works differently when you are reading words on paper instead of on a screen. Books are much longer and more in-depth than any clickbait Internet article. Reading a book means taking the time to explore issues, questions, and obstacles fully, so you get a well-rounded picture of the situation, not a bite-sized summary.

Books are strange and fresh, and subversive by nature, because they ask us to imagine worlds and realities that are different from our own; that is inherently subversive, imagination stretching, and therefore reality stretching. To read is to imagine another way, therefore to read is to protest. Read an inspiring book! Here is a list of recommendations to get you started.

NONFICTION

Requiem for the American Dream, Noam Chomsky

Chomsky gives a conversational, sharp, and in-depth analysis of the ten principles of concentration of wealth and power, to show exactly how wealth inequality has shaped democracy throughout history to get us to where we are today. He lays out how the oligarchy has consciously and concertedly pushed back in reaction to the progress of the '60s to concentrate wealth and power in the hands of the people Adam Smith called the "masters of mankind."

The Diary of Anne Frank, Anne Frank

The diary of a young Jewish girl, written in hiding during Hitler's Nazi occupation of Holland. Beautiful and heartbreaking. Books like this are so important because they take something like the Holocaust, which can seem like an impersonal number, a blurry historic fact, and make it personal. Anne Frank's diary reminds us that racist fascism hurts real people.

The Captive Mind, Czeslaw Milosz

The Czech poet details what it is like as an artist and an intellectual to live within a country that has fallen prey to an oppressive regime. Milosz (who also wrote some very wonderful poetry) describes the different ways that people can lie to themselves in order to accept an authoritarian regime.

On Tyranny, Timothy Snyder

You can get a lot of knowledge in a short amount of time with this book; it's a fast read, lucid and concise. Shows what we can learn from history about how to resist the methods and tactics of fascism. Lays out the many parallels between tyrants of the past century and the current president.

Indivisible

OK, this one isn't really a book. It's a free online manifesto that was quickly put together in the days after the 2016 election by some policy wonks who worked in the Obama administration. They point out how effective the Tea Party's tactics of putting pressure on local politics was, and explain how to use those same tactics against the Trump administration. You can read the whole thing in the time it takes to brew and drink a cup of tea.

(Download the PDF at indivisible.com.)

Persepolis, Marjane Satrapi

This graphic novel tells the real-life story of young Marjane growing up in the 1980s and experiencing her homeland of Iran being taken over by an oppressive regime. Entertaining, and beautifully illustrated, it shows what it was like to go from a society with intellectual and cultural freedom to one of oppression.

A People's History of the United States, Howard Zinn

Zinn demonstrates that in history, time and again, change only happens when people can set aside their differences and stand together against rich people who use politics to make sure they stay rich and in power. For young adults there is also Zinn's *A Young People's History of the United States*, which is slightly shorter and has the added bonus of showing historical episodes where young people made an impact as activists.

Civil Disobedience, Henry David Thoreau

Thoreau argues that we should listen to what our conscience tells us, not what the government legislates. Thoreau refused to pay his taxes to a government that supported slavery. He believed when the law of the land is immoral it is up to the individual to take a stand for what he knows to be right.

Listen, Liberal, Thomas Frank

Thomas Frank is always provocative and fun to read, I'm a fan. Here Frank asks what went wrong with the Democratic Party. He demonstrates that historically the Democratic Party was the party of the common people, the party fighting for workers and fighting for social justice, and the Democratic Party can only regain its health if it returns to those roots—and becomes the party of the working class and not of Wall Street.

Hope in the Dark, Rebecca Solnit

An argument that being progressive does not mean being stuck in the gloomy mindset of dystopian apocalyptic bummers. Solnit shares examples of hope, from her experience as an activist to stories of the Zapatistas, the WTO protests, the American civil rights movement, and the fall of the Berlin Wall.

FICTION

Parable of the Sower and *Parable of the Talents*, Octavia E. Butler

Set in the not-too-distant 2024, Butler's *Parable* novels show us the trajectory of our world with climate change and corporate power left unchecked. An African American teenager fights for survival in a world where the sea is rising, water is scarce, fires rampage across California, schools and cities are privat-

ized, and the homeless are kept at bay by walls. People escape
the horrors of reality with designer drugs and addictive virtual
realities. In this dystopia, a politician rises up whose religious
followers commit violent atrocities in a crusade to hold on to
the past. His slogan: Make America Great Again.

Nineteen Eighty-Four, George Orwell

A book about the power of tyranny in modern times that
illustrates the frightening power of modern propaganda, where
"War is peace, freedom is slavery, ignorance is strength."

Animal Farm, George Orwell

The pigs in charge of the farm sell off Boxer, the hardworking
horse, to be slaughtered, and use the money to buy themselves
whiskey. What better analogy for the Republicans defunding
people's health care, in order to give the rich tax cuts?

The Handmaid's Tale, Margaret Atwood

A chilling depiction of a world of repression, where women
are property, nonwhites have been relocated to a segregated
zone, and a fundamentalist interpretation of the Bible informs
all politics. Mike Pence would probably describe it differently.

For Whom the Bell Tolls, Ernest Hemingway

A sweeping work of resistance and the human spirit. Hem-
ingway captures something about the weight, and value, and
beauty of life itself (as all great novels do) that is particularly

inspiring here in the story of people fighting against fascism during the Spanish Civil War.

....
There is a reason why oppressive
regimes ban books, not guns.
....

7.
DON'T FORGET THIS
PRESIDENT IS A MORON

Stupid is as stupid does.

—Forrest Gump

ACTION

Don't forget that Trump is incredibly
ignorant and stupid.

RESULT

An awareness of what we are dealing with.

There has often been this desire by the media, columnists, and talking heads to paint President Trump as being cunning, and clever. He is not. Let's not make this overly complicated; Donald Trump is a total moron.

How did this idiot beat all the other candidates? Trump is the terminal point of feeding half the nation a toxic stew of lies, conspiracy theories, and a rhetoric of fear. Trump is a lucky idiot.

"I have a very good brain and I've said lots of things."

—D. Trump

The president has the attention span of a drunk fruit fly. White House aides say when they give him briefing memos they have to insert his own name into security briefings to hold his attention! When he goes to foreign countries, leaders are told to keep speeches two to four minutes long, so they don't overload him with information or lose his interest.

Incredibly, Trump's stupidity is part of his appeal. He has dumb, simple ideas. Ban all Muslims. Build a wall. Bomb North Korea. These are the kind of ideas that would occur to a child. That makes them easy to stick in the minds of ignorant voters. Unfortunately, they are also incredibly dumbed-down, oversimplified approaches to complicated problems. Trump's dumbness is his appeal to his base; they understand him because stupid is never complicated, it's simple and easy to understand. It also doesn't get much accomplished, because reality is more complicated than a sound-bite slogan. Or as Trump said: "Nobody knew health care could be so complicated."

We have to take the real, pressing, and complicated issues like health care, global warming, immigration, and global terrorist threats, and figure out how to explain our solutions and tactics for handling these problems in simple ways, in ways that even a fourth grader can understand, because otherwise too many people will go with the oversimplified versions offered by idiots like Trump. I'm not trying to insult the intelligence of the American people. I think it's actually more a matter of there being so much going on in the world today, from science, to politics, to culture and technology; it's impossible for anyone to be an expert in all of it. That's why we need experts, people who specialize in a given area, but we need the ideas of experts to be accessible to all. Enough people have to be familiar enough with the facts to recognize Trump for the dunce he is. Trump is a dingbat, a knuckledragger, a cretinous clown, a laughing-stock, a moronic airhead, a self-obsessed bimbo.

Idiotic Warmongering with North Korea

While the fact that Trump is a loudmouth halfwit reminds us we can outsmart him, we must also keep in mind the serious danger that comes from having a dumb man-child in charge of a situation as beyond his understanding as running a country or handling international diplomacy. He is incredibly out of his depth, and this fact should remind us why resistance to Trump is so important. Leaving an idiot in charge of foreign policy is a dangerous game. Perhaps nothing demonstrates this better than Trump's warmongering with North Korea. Then he does a complete about-face and says he's willing to have direct talks with Kim Jong-un. Since Trump is neither a man of peace nor diplomacy, I would not hold out much hope for those direct talks.

Trump's stupid and belligerent pestering of North Korea could very well bring about a completely unnecessary war where thousands of lives are lost. If the US attacked North Korea the imbalance of force would lead to a devastating and inhumane global catastrophe. With North Korea's potential development of nuclear missiles, Trump's ham-fisted handling of a delicate situation threatens to set off a nuclear conflict. Direct talks will not help matters unless Trump can conduct them with genuine good faith, which is almost impossible to imagine.

Threatening violence is never the best option for solving anything, and direct talks would normally be the right thing to do, but it is hard to imagine Trump accomplishing anything that way, although a different leader could. Calling the unpredictable dictator of a foreign nation "short and fat" is historically bad statecraft, to put it mildly. North Korea has offered to suspend their nuclear testing program if America agreed to stop running war games in South Korea. China has also backed this strategy. These war games are a needless provocation. Trump's strategy for handling North Korea is like pestering a small but dangerous rattlesnake. Rather than seek a peaceful solution, Trump continually fans the flames and raises the possibility of starting a fire that could quickly spread out of control and cause unimaginable violence and damage. It's a tragedy in the making, that this man is in control of the military and of the nuclear launch codes.

Trump has threatened North Korea repeatedly, making ominous threats like "they may not be around much longer." In 2017, they famously began engaging in insults, like the pair of overgrown fifth-grade bullies they are, with Trump calling Kim "Rocket Man," and Kim calling Trump "mentally deranged US dotard." Is this what international diplomacy has come to? We need grown-ups to take charge.

It would be funny if it were not so scary, we are watching these reckless adult men bluster like idiotic drunks before a bar fight, but the stakes are the lives of hundreds of thousands, thermonuclear war, and conceivably a global war. Remember that it only took the shooting of the duke of a small Austro-Hungarian country to spark off World War I. Who knows the ultimate consequences at stake if the United States becomes involved in a military invasion of North Korea, all because our elected leader can't stop tweeting third-grader-level insults. If anything, this should serve as a reminder of how big the stakes are for our resistance and how every day matters when it comes to the safety of everyone alive.

Foreign Policy Damages

It would be difficult for a president to do more damage to America's standing and reputation on the international stage if they tried. Trump attacks allies who have faithfully sided with the United States since World War II, while praising dictators past and present like Rodrigo Duterte, Bashar al-Assad, Muammar Gaddafi, and Saddam Hussein. While American officials say Putin's Russia is America's largest geopolitical threat, Trump praises Putin constantly. Gestures such as this have long-term, serious political consequences.

Every single nation in the world is a part of the Paris climate accord to fight climate change except for America, because of Donald Trump. Trump ended any chance of America brokering peace in the Middle East by going against decades of American policy and recognizing Jerusalem as the capital of Israel. Trump tried to shake down NATO members for payments as if America were running a mafia protection racket. He decertified the Iran deal, which allies and the US had negotiated to stop Iran from developing nuclear weapons. He has weakened our relationship with long-term allies, such as Germany. Once we were seen as the foundation of the international, peace-oriented order. Now we are seen as an unpredictable loose cannon.

While Trump's petulant strongman baby act may fool his base, it is not fooling anyone on the global stage. German officials find Trump's lack of basic foreign knowledge frightening, and it seems the president cannot meet with a foreign leader without embarrassing the office of the president, yanking and squeezing the hands of foreign leaders like an insecure loser, shoving international leaders like an uncivilized thug, and undercutting American diplomacy and international policy with his Diet Coke–fueled Twitter binges. Foreign leaders realize that despite his bluster, it is surprisingly easy to get the better end of the deal when negotiating with Trump; all that is necessary is to impress him with flattery, a military parade, or some shiny object. Republican politicians who excuse this behavior try to act as if the words of the president don't matter—which is untrue. For example, Trump offended America's closest ally, Britain, by tweeting inflammatory anti-Muslim hate propaganda videos taken from a fringe ultranationalist British hate group, supposedly showing Muslims committing acts of violence, such as a video entitled "Muslim migrant beats up Dutch boy on crutches," when in fact the assailant was neither Muslim nor a migrant. When Britain's leader condemned Trump for spreading hate, the president then attacked her on Twitter as well. Because he is a giant ass.

Which is why Britain and other world leaders see Trump for what he is, even if a quarter of our own population cannot. It will take years, and much work, to undo the damage caused by this presidency to America's place in the world. As David Lammy, member of the British Parliament, wrote, "The President of the United States is promoting a fascist, racist, extremist hate group whose leaders have been arrested and convicted. He is no ally or friend of ours." It is important that we let our allies know we too recognize Trump for what he truly is: an idiot.

Allen Ginsberg by Martha Grover

8.

GUARD FREEDOM OF
THE PRESS

I suppose the most revolutionary act one can
engage in is . . . to tell the truth.
—Howard Zinn

ACTION
Find yourself a good source of real news.

RESULT
Support the press while keeping yourself informed.

President Trump frequently calls the press the "enemy of the American people." It's hard to overstate how crazy that is. For our country's president to declare the entire profession that is supposed to be the watchdog protecting our civil rights our enemy is the kind of announcement you'd expect from a conspiracy-addled crackpot or a dictator, but when it comes from the president, it must be understood as an attempt to undermine truth itself, and our country's ability to navigate truth. Tyrants always attack journalists, newspapers, and the truth; it is the most surefire sign that we are dealing with a would-be tyrant. On February 14, 2017, in a private conversation, Trump urged James Comey, the FBI director, to throw journalists in jail. As of this writing that has not taken place, but that doesn't mean we're safe. He would do it if he thought he could get away with it.

We have all seen how this president is hell-bent on creating an alternate reality for himself and his followers; it is part of his bullshit spell. The antidote begins with you: make sure that you yourself are well informed of the facts. As with all the tactics and strategies in this book, we must start with ourselves. This principle of activism is based on the simple but profound idea of Mahatma Gandhi, that we must as individuals be the change we wish to see in the world.

If there is a canary in the coal mine that alerts people to tyranny, it is the president's war against the media. Any fact or opinion that he does not like he declares "fake news." His counselors speak "alternative facts." This is an assault on logic, on reason, on facts, and on truth. Without truth we are lost. As historian Timothy Snyder has written, "Post-Truth is pre-fascism."

Trump declaring war on the press was the first step in his campaign to bully and weaken the media in America. He wants the American public to believe what he says, not what the facts are. For many Americans, giving up their own ability to track complicated news and issues, and trust instead in the posturing lies of a leader who is always right no matter what, is seductive. In the world of authoritarianism, there is no questioning, there is no doubt; the fearless leader is always correct. Things are simpler that way. The complexity of the world can be reduced to a mindless faith in the strongman leader. The authoritarian leader is only safe when, no matter what crazy bullshit he says, he is believed. Kim Jong-un tells his nation that he does not poop, and they believe him. Also, Kim Jong-un could drive at age three and his dad invented hamburgers.

Like North Korea's dictator, Trump's specialty is to lie continuously, at such a rapid pace that fact-checkers just can't keep up. For years Trump kept a book of Hitler's speeches next to his bed; it seems he learned a big lesson from Hitler, who wrote: "Make the lie big, make it simple, keep saying it, and eventually they will believe it."

Saying that those who disagree with them are unpatriotic is another card tyrants love to play. Dissent is dangerous. Under Stalin, the state controlled what people read in a very simple manner: books and articles disagreeing with what the government sanctioned as "true" were banned. Any writers who insisted on voicing disagreement were punished by being thrown in jail.

Today, that kind of censorship no longer works quite as well (yet). The modern difference being the Internet. It is harder to ban blogs and websites than it was to ban books. Which makes the repeal of net neutrality all the more ominous. As the media has evolved, the tactics that an oppressive regime uses to silence dissent have also evolved. In Putin's Russia, the media is controlled by the Kremlin. Not only are journalists who dare report the truth harassed, threatened, and jailed, the modern authoritarian strategy also involves muddying the media waters with disinformation. Ultimately it is also quite possible for a modern authoritarian government to censor the Internet, which is what they do in China.

With the Internet, we now have a larger quantity of information, but the quality is pretty hit-or-miss. In fact a lot of it is garbage. Sadly, many people who can't tell the difference between real and fake news lack media literacy. The long-term strategy to defend against this muddying of the waters is to promote media literacy in schools. Ideally, every high school grad should be able to tell the difference between a factually based article and a steaming heap of mistruth from Breitbart, etc.

We can fix this problem in two ways. We can make people smarter at figuring out what is real and what is fake news. Or we make real fake news easier to spot—by requiring entertainment and opinion to be labeled as such. The best solution is to use both of these strategies. Those are the long-term strategies. The specific tactic of this book is to start with yourself, and make sure you are getting a regular dose of actual, factual news from diverse sources.

Diversify Your News

The most dangerous thing to a fortress of lies is an army of people who know the facts. We need smart, savvy, well-informed, media-literate citizens. Support journalism. An easy way to do that is to buy a newspaper. But don't stop there! I encourage you to go deeper, there are a lot of great sources of news that go beyond the basic media diet of the front page. Many of the resources listed below exist as websites that you can support by signing up for a membership. Here are a dozen places you should check out to diversify your info diet.

Regular Old Newspapers (Available from newsstands or on your front porch.)

The *New York Times*, the *Washington Post*, etc. are good places to start. In the media food pyramid think of this as one of the basic building blocks of a healthy diet and then branch out.

Mother Jones (motherjones.com)

An award-winning nonprofit magazine that covers politics and the environment from a perspective that is more aggressive and critical of corruption than mainstream newspapers generally are. In an age when news media is often owned by a corporation that has a vested interest in what gets printed, nonprofit news organizations matter more than ever.

The *Nation* (thenation.com)

The oldest and most widely read weekly progressive magazine in the US, the *Nation* is one place where you can get the news from journalists who don't have to report under the constraint of nonpartisanship, which normalizes the insanity of having a petulant baby-man like Trump as our president.

Jacobin (jacobinmag.com)

Proudly radical and socialist commentary on the news. This is democratic socialism with a modern and accessible style. Noam Chomsky calls this magazine "a bright light in dark times."

The *Guardian* (theguardian.com)

A British daily newspaper, very useful for getting an international perspective on what is going on in the USA. It has won multiple accolades, including ranking first on openness and accountability in a study on global news outlets.

ProPublica (propublica.org)

A nonprofit newsroom that's dedicated to journalism in the public interest. They state their mission as "to expose abuses of power." In other words, news not just as a source of entertainment but that's meant to help us make better decisions as a society.

Talking Points Memo (talkingpointsmemo.com)

Savvy news analysis that goes beyond the front page. If you want a better understanding of what is going on, from a decidedly liberal perspective that never feels ham-fisted or melodramatic, I recommend TPM as a frequent stop on your Internet travels.

The Rachel Maddow Show (TV)

If you are someone who prefers to watch the news, this is a nightly television show (also available as a radio program and podcast) with a liberal take on the news that is as wonky and in-depth as it is cheeky and entertaining.

Democracy Now! with Amy Goodman (Radio)

An hour-long alternative radio show (check your local listings) that examines current affairs from the perspective of social change. This show has plenty of die-hard fans. In Portland, Oregon, this is often what's on the radio in informed people's kitchens in the afternoons.

Robert Reich's Resistance Report (Facebook)

Speaking of other news formats, here is somebody that is well worth following on Facebook. Robert Reich offers a daily *Resistance Report* that consists of a short video analyzing the news. As a former cabinet member of Bill Clinton and an early supporter of Bernie Sanders he has his own take on the resistance that is clear-eyed but also hopeful. He has been stalwart in warning people of the dangers of Donald Trump and sharing important ways people can push back.

Pod Save America (Download from iTunes)

There are a lot of great podcasts out there. The guys behind *Pod Save America* bust down the latest dumb sh!t from Trump-land with plenty of swearing, humor, and insight. The foul-mouthed hosts are former political aides to Barack Obama so they have plenty of insight into the inside baseball of politics.

Late-Night Comedy (TV or just YouTube it)

There is no reason you can't laugh while staying informed. The satire found on these shows is way funnier than anything that right-wing media will ever come up with and we should celebrate that. Pick whichever one makes you laugh the most. Lord knows we need it. Check out shows like *Last Week Tonight with John Oliver*, *The Late Show with Stephen Colbert*, *Full Frontal with Samantha Bee*, *Late Night with Seth Meyers*, and *The Daily Show with Trevor Noah*.

Independent Bookstores (In real life)

This is going to vary from town to town, but most decent-sized cities have a bookstore that is knowledgeable and committed to sharing ideas, news, and information beyond the front-page news cycle. Figure out what is close to you and connect with them. Yes, talking to informed people in real life is a great way to stay informed! Who knows where it might lead?

....

When the truth is under attack, being
informed is resistance.

....

9.

UNPLUG: AVOID MEDIA BURNOUT

Men have become the tools of their tools.
—Henry David Thoreau

ACTION

Take a break from the reality TV White House
show, the news, TV, and the Internet once
in a while. Find balance.

RESULT

Greater focus, energy, and clarity.
Safeguard against burnout.

There is a balance between ignoring what is going on altogether, and immersing ourselves in the toxic onslaught
of bad news to the point that it's overwhelming. Where you
strike that balance is going to be a little different for everyone.
Just like finding the right diet of food for your body, everybody is going to have different concerns and needs for what is
a healthy media diet for themselves, and when to break from
it. There is no one-size-fits-all daily news schedule that is right

for everyone. Instead, you should come up with your own idea about how to limit your news-cycle intake to the right amount for you.

Here are some suggestions or starting points to consider.
- Make one day a week news free.
- Even better, make one day a week Internet free.
- Or at least make one day a week a Trump-free day.
- Avoid news before bedtime. For example, if you go to bed at midnight, consider giving yourself a no news after 10 p.m. rule.
- Some combination of the above.

I try to do two things: I have a media-free day, one day each weekend where I try to avoid news and the Internet altogether. It's my media detox day. I also avoid getting on the Internet late at night (I make the cut off midnight) because that's when I am most prone to get sucked into the never-ending stream of news, clicking on article after article.

Outrage exhaustion is a real tactic the Republican regime uses. We already know too well what a monster he is, there is no need to tire ourselves out reconfirming this endlessly. Instead, we should only keep tabs on his agenda insofar as it helps us combat that agenda.

I'm not saying you shouldn't feel outrage. The corrupt administration is well deserving of outrage and scorn, but don't let that emotion wear you out. Let your energy come from the strength of the goodness in your heart, let your positive desire for truth and what is right motivate you as much as anything else!

It's all about balance. Striking the balance of emotions so that, yeah, you remain angry when Trump does something reprehensible and use that to keep your head in the game, to fight against apathy. But remember, your ability to resist is built upon your desire for freedom and truth.

....
This is going to be a marathon, not a sprint.
....

10.

BEWARE OF NORMALIZATION

Whoever is careless with the truth in small matters
cannot be trusted with important matters.
—Albert Einstein

ACTION

Write a short note to yourself about what you believe
and why it is worth fighting for; use this to avoid the
normalization of Trump.

RESULT

Strengthening your awareness of what is good and
true, and building an immunity against what isn't.

The important thing to remember is that this is not our way of life! And we cannot let ourselves come to accept it. Imagine if every day your next-door neighbor took a crap in the middle of the street, like an untrained dog. That would be, among many other things, highly unacceptable. If this went on day after day and nothing were done to stop it, the whole neighborhood might just come to accept this behavior. That's the process of normalization—it's allowing the absurd and the unacceptable to become accepted by force of repetition.

Part of "normalization" is to cast about trying to paint the situation in a different light, as if the president weren't the terrible, racist, misogynistic, completely incompetent nutjob that he is. Normalization is the desire to say "oh, this isn't so bad." Normalization is saying "this is fine" while your house burns.

Normalization is the same process that makes us want to not look at the racism and sexism that is at large, and possibly growing, in our national psyche, because it is ugly.

America came down with a bad case of the demagogue, because our normally healthy immune system was weak. A big part of the immune system that I am referring to is our news, but it also includes our civic culture. The first step to healing is not to ignore that you are sick, it is to recognize the severity of the infection so that you can fight it. The action of this chapter is to write a note to yourself, listing all the ways that Trump's presidency isn't normal. Take it out and add to it whenever you need to. I recommend taking a look at it on a regular basis; this alone will be enough to remind you that having a guy like Trump as president is anything but normal.

....

A conman, pussy-grabbing, bigoted, self-obsessed, vain, old grifter for president is NOT normal.

....

11.

PRAYER AND MEDITATION

Where there is peace and meditation, there is neither anxiety nor doubt.
—St. Francis de Sales

ACTION

Pray or meditate.

RESULT

Spiritual strength.

I believe this is a spiritual battle as much as it is a political one. Can we again become a country of freedom, of religious liberty, a country where the truth is respected? Or will we continue to be a country where people are judged according to their religion, where people are treated differently because of their skin color? Are we going to become a country where the fringe ideas of the alt-right become more and more commonplace? Or will we ever be a nation of compassion and fairness for everyone, regardless of their skin color, regardless of their faith and beliefs?

We stand at a crossroads. We as a people will decide whether we remain a place that values freedom and equality, or trade those in for nationalism and the protection of an authoritarian—who protects us from the bogeymen he creates. Equality and freedom are things that we now must fight for, and this fight demands we engage on every level, including the spiritual.

This struggle is not simply one of logic and emotions, it is something bigger. This is the fight of our lifetimes, a crossroads that may only come along every few generations.

Let us engage in this profound fight with everything we have, let us do so because we recognize how much is at stake—the future of freedom, equality, and democracy itself. We fight for what we hold sacred. Because of this I say the Resistance is spiritual, not just politics as usual.

Whatever your spiritual practice may be, now is the time to use it. Let each of us embrace the best that our traditions have to offer, and let each of us strive to make our beliefs give us strength to impact this world, positively, for the world needs compassion and healing now as much as it ever has.

Loving-Kindness Meditation

In case you are not quite sure how to approach this idea of spirituality as a form of resistance, here is an easy and effective meditation practice you can try for the action of this chapter. It's called *metta* or loving-kindness meditation. It comes from the Dalai Lama, who practices it every day and is probably the practice's best-known proponent. It is essentially an exercise used to increase empathy, to open up to the world and to others. It can be done in just a few minutes. It is quite simple and easy, since it simply consists of saying this sentence: "May you be happy, may you be healthy, may you be free of pain," while thinking of three different people, one after the other. Loving-kindness meditation is about directing goodwill toward others. That's it.

Here is how you do it:

Sit in a comfortable position. Start by thinking of someone that you already feel compassion toward while saying (out loud or in your head), "May you be happy, may you be healthy, may you be free from pain." Repeat this three times.

Next, you repeat this but directed toward someone you feel neutral about. It could be anyone, an acquaintance, someone from work, or a person you saw crossing the street today. The idea is that by wishing good health and well-being toward a neutral person you stretch and strengthen your empathy muscles, making you stronger and more flexible.

Finally you can take it a step further, when you are ready, and direct this same loving-kindness toward someone who is a difficult person for you. It could be someone you had an argument with, or it could be someone you have trouble getting along with, or even a bully you fought with in third grade. You get the idea. And yes, you could even direct this loving-kindness toward someone you disagree with politically! Loving-kindness is about expanding the circle of empathy and goodwill that all of us have naturally to include everybody.

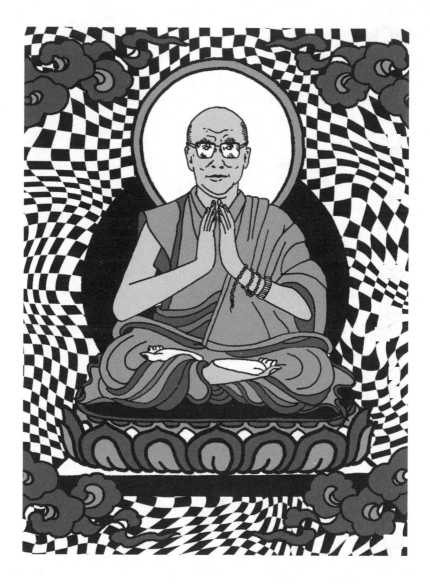

The Dalai Lama by Emma Bagley

12

SAVOR EVERYDAY LIFE

In the depth of winter I finally learned that there lay
within me an invincible summer.
—Albert Camus

ACTION
Use the fears and the worries of this era to
inspire a deeper appreciation for all the things
that are worth fighting for.

RESULT
A new outlook.

The day after Trump was elected I went for a walk in my neighborhood, down streets that I have known since I was a kid, and everything looked different; the familiar streets, the people of Portland, the light and the air itself, and I realized the difference was in me, in how I was seeing everything. There was a sweetness and a light to everyday life that was there because it is fragile, because nothing is guaranteed. Safety from a nuclear war breaking out is not guaranteed, the march of progress in the name of freedom and equality is not a given, basic human rights, all of this, democratic civilization itself, and the future, it is all so fragile. Realizing that made me appreciate it, and perhaps this was the inspiration to write this book, knowing that what we do have is worth fighting for, and seeing it threatened made me value it all that much more.

So, here we are, with a supremely ignorant, blustering charlatan in charge of the country, steering the ship right off a cliff. We are at the mercy of the whims of a bragging, thin-skinned idiot.

The very basic foundations of America are under attack. Anything and everything is up in the air. That very uncertainty and the danger that Trump presents should in fact make us live life with stronger appreciation than ever before, because it is easy now to see how much we have taken for granted.

Where do we go from here? I wish I wasn't writing this book. I bet you have better things to do than to continually worry about the fact that the president is an incompetent racist with a urine fetish, and who is very possibly in bed with Russia. It's not what any of us want to spend our free time thinking about, or worrying about. And yet, to just ignore all of this—to ignore the tides of racism, to ignore this administration's devastating effect on the environment and the Republicans' ceaseless efforts to strip millions of people of their health care, this president's outspoken approval and emboldening of white supremacy, his blatant sexism, his blathering idiocy, his dangerous warmongering with North Korea, his endless attacks on minorities and those he perceives to be different or weak, and the precedent this sets—to ignore the clear and present danger he presents to democracy would be irresponsible. It would be irresponsible not only to ourselves but to future generations and to past generations.

For much of my life I have felt like my generation sort of missed out on history. Nothing much was happening, it seemed. There seemed to be this unspoken assumption that progress was inevitable and would happen on its own without our having to do much if anything to keep it on track. Somehow, when I look back at the past decade, it is as if we became afraid to evolve, to change. It seemed the present was tired of trying to come up with anything new; instead it felt like we as a culture were just kind of treading water, waiting for something to happen.

Now we know that if we don't take the reins and create, then someone else will. It turns out that the nation as a whole was surprisingly ready for a new direction, for change. Real change is the only way forward, in fact it is unavoidable, but will it be Trump's America or a different vision that wins out? Whichever it is, we know that we can no longer tread water, staying in an unchanging version of 2015. History will march on with or without us. It is time to fight for everything you believe in and hold dear.

Resistance Accomplishments

It is well worth keeping in mind the positive impact that the Resistance has had so far. Without people raising their voices—to protest, to make phone calls, to push back against this administration's agenda—things would be far worse. We should take heart, knowing that the mobilization and action of Team Resistance has a direct impact in limiting the damage done by this administration. As Senator Bernie Sanders put it: "The silver lining of the Trump administration is that millions of people are getting involved in politics for the first time to fight back."

This administration did not have a good first year, to put it mildly. Despite Trump and his cronies being in control of the government, they have met with outspoken resistance at every turn. Trump's polls are in the toilet and sinking. The tax scam, the one piece of legislation they were able to push through, is immensely unpopular, and it will exact a heavy price in lost votes in the next election cycle. Trump's travel ban was overturned by the courts, not once but twice. The White House has been plagued by unprecedented leaks since day one, and whistleblowers throughout every government agency have fought to keep the public aware of what is really going on. Trump's inauguration was met with the Women's March—the largest single-day protest in US history! This dysfunctional administration has been continuously and spectacularly imploding with an unprecedented swath of resignations, including that of chief strategist Steve Bannon, national security adviser Michael Flynn, alt-right nutjob Sebastian Gorka, communications director Anthony Scaramucci, chief of staff Reince Priebus, and press secretary Sean Spicer to name just a few. Four people involved with Trump's administration have been indicted on criminal charges—Michael Flynn, George Papadopoulos, Paul Manafort, and Richard Gates—and that's surely just the beginning. The Resistance also mobilized to stop Trump from being able to repeal Obamacare, in large part by making enough phone calls to Congress to scare off the Republicans from voting to repeal it. The people are on the move, and the White House is in a continuous meltdown mode—even as they sneak through harmful policy changes. The moral is clear—we must keep the pressure on! It is also well worth remembering that the damage being done by this administration can be undone. A prime example of this is the Paris climate accord, which Trump would pull America out of, but that change does not actually take place until 2020. If Trump is no longer president, pulling out of the Paris accord will never happen.

There are moments in history that are pivotal, moments when the course of a nation is chosen. As Shakespeare put it, "There is a tide in the affairs of men, which taken at the flood, leads on to fortune." I believe that right now is our moment in history, the moment future generations will look back on and see a time when everyday people became heroes. This moment in history is your chance to bring to bear the best of everything that you are and that you have within you. This is the fight of our generation.

PART 2
FIGHT!

Harvey Milk by Erin Nations

13.

GROW YOUR GRASSROOTS: FIGHT LOCALLY

History is instructive. And what it suggests to people is that even if they do little things, if they walk on the picket line, if they join a vigil, if they write a letter to their local newspaper. Anything they do, however small, becomes part of a much, much larger sort of flow of energy. And when enough people do enough things, however s mall they are, then change takes place.

—Howard Zinn

ACTION
Find a way to join the Resistance by starting locally, right where you live.

RESULT
Strength in unity.

G rassroots action is the slow-growing roots of a plant that appear small but are strong enough to tear apart concrete. Grassroots action is based upon the knowledge that the actions, the choices, the words of people like you and me can add up to something huge. Rosa Parks was not trying to begin the snowball that led to the end of segregation when she refused to give up her seat and move to the back of the bus, she was just making one small courageous choice in her own life.

To harness the power of grassroots action is to recognize that together the millions of drops of water make up an unstoppable wave.

....
Start where you are and start today.
....

Wherever you live right now, take a moment and ask yourself, How can I get involved locally? There are a handful of Resistance groups that sprang up in the aftermath of the Trump election, and you should look to see what your local options are. One place that seems to be doing a good job of spreading is the group Indivisible. Another is the ACLU. The Democratic Socialists of America have seen a spike in new members that tripled their numbers since the 2016 election and more than half of the new members are people under thirty. People are starting to wake up and realize that we have everything to fight for and the time and the place to step up and get involved is here and now.

You could join the fight in raising awareness about global warming. Or maybe you are down the street from a homeless shelter and you want to see if they need volunteers. Sign petitions. Go to protest marches. Get involved in local government; that affects what happens on the national stage. Focus on what is at hand, near you, and you can transform the feelings of frustration that Trump provokes into positive action, right where you live. Don't underestimate the power of changing the world locally.

I'm inspired by a local hero, someone you have probably never heard of if you don't live in Portland—Chloe Eudaly. For years Chloe ran a rad little independent bookstore in downtown Portland called Reading Frenzy. Portland has been undergoing crazy gentrification, and landlords have been tightening the screws on renters all across our city, raising the rent 100 percent in a matter of months on some people. A lot of my friends have had to move away because their rents doubled in the course of a year. Chloe's store had to relocate when her rent was raised. But what finally did it for her was noticing an ad on Craigslist; someone was renting out the garden shed in their backyard, as housing, for a ridiculous price.

For Chloe, that was the last straw. So she ran for public office. She ran for city council exclusively on the platform of fighting the out-of-control rent. She ran against a much more experienced incumbent politician, and against all odds, she won! Local politics saw it as a huge upset, as though she had come out of nowhere—but the real reason she won is because she was talking about what people cared about locally.

14.

YOU ARE THE BOSS: CALL YOUR PUBLIC SERVANT

We the people are the rightful masters of both Congress and the courts, not to overthrow the Constitution but to overthrow the men who pervert the Constitution.

—Abraham Lincoln

ACTION

Call your member of Congress and tell
them what to do.

RESULT

Lets your local politician, who works for you, know
what you want them to do and that you will be
keeping an eye on them and voting accordingly.

Republicans' multiple attempts to repeal Obamacare have failed spectacularly (at least three times) because people resisted, they got involved, they got organized, they made phone calls and pressured Congress not to pass legislation that would have stripped millions of Americans of health care. This is a major victory for the Resistance, one that demonstrates the power we have when we fight back. Members of the Resistance—were relentless in applying the necessary pressure to stop Trump dead in his tracks on one of his central campaign promises. People organized and made hundreds of thousands of phone calls to senators and fellow constituents in key states to kill so-called Trumpcare, it didn't just fail because of GOP incompetence (although that certainly helped). The lesson here is that when we organize and apply tenacious pressure we are the ones who call the shots. (On the heels of their defeat, they've been searching for and finding other ways to undermine Obamacare by reducing funding, so stay on guard.)

Every senator cares a heck of a lot more about their own reelection than Trump's. The most direct way to push against Trump's agenda is to put pressure on your local and state representatives. One easy way to do that is to call them up and let them know exactly how you feel about the job they are doing. Sometimes it's easy to think—someone else can do this, so I don't have to. Don't make that mistake—take advantage of the simple but powerful action of making that phone call.

If you haven't already, you might consider saving this number to your phone: 202-224-3121. That's the number for the United States Capitol Hill switchboard, and from there you can reach the office of every single senator and congressperson. Give them an earful! That number will literally get hold of all of them, but you can also reach out locally by contacting your local district office. As with all forms of resistance, keep in mind this is a marathon not a sprint. Phone calls are important but don't tire yourself out, seek a balance with this activity and using all the tools of resistance at your disposal.

You don't have to limit yourself to phone calls with this action. You can find out if your representative has a local office and pay them a visit. Find out when the next town hall meeting is. Think of it like you would going to a parent-teacher meeting, or a neighborhood safety meeting. Governors, senators, mayors, and other elected officials have offices and contact information that are set up to hear what you have to say.

A friend of mine used to work as an intern in the office of a

....

The politicians work for you, be a boss!

....

senator. One of his main jobs was to answer the phone for the senator's office and keep a tally of what people called in about. The senator would get that information every day, and you better believe he paid close attention to it. Why? Because the senator wanted to get reelected, and he knew that the people calling in and praising him for voting the way they wanted, or chewing him out when he voted against their wishes, were the same people that decided if he got to keep his job.

The Tea Party did a great job of using this to their advantage. They were merciless to their representatives. They made demands, they showed up at town halls, they got the attention of their public officials, and they shifted the national political dialogue in the direction they wanted. By stealing a page from the Tea Party, we can make sure that our representatives hear us loud and clear. The Tea Party had outside help, hundreds of millions of dollars' worth of help, from the Koch family. But the tactics work with or without that level of funding. In fact the battle at hand is to a large degree going to be a fight between Big Money and Big Hearts. Who do you want to win that fight?

It's certainly not like the Tea Party invented the playbook on how to pressure politicians! Putting pressure on politicians is what the progressive movement was built upon. We have many tools at our disposal, from strikes and protests to boycotts and marches, but if we are going to do all of that, why skip the easiest and most obvious?

I encourage you to check out a great guide on how to most effectively put pressure on your member of Congress. It is free online and came out soon after Trump's election, it's the Indivisible Guide—Indivisible was a major force in shutting down the attempts to repeal health care. You can find it at indivisbleguide.com. It's a PDF that's twenty-six pages long and breaks down how and why putting pressure on local politicians works. I sincerely encourage you to check it out (it was written by a bunch of wonky political folks, so they know the skinny on how to pressure politicians), but here is a quick summary as well.

The main ideas:

Organize locally, and pressure local politicians for best results.

Your MOC (member of Congress) has a number-one priority, getting reelected. Use this to make them listen and act.

Get their attention by going to town halls, public events, visiting their district office and asking for a meeting, and making calls in coordination with local groups.

Make your voice heard. It would be silly for us to complain about how much Trump sucks and yet not use our voices to speak out in the simplest and most effective way available to us.

Cesar Chavez by Zack Soto

15.
PROTEST!

Those who profess to favor freedom, and yet deprecate agitation, are men who want crops without plowing up the ground.
—Frederick Douglass

ACTION
Protest! Strap on your marching boots
and hit the streets.

RESULT
You raise awareness and strengthen solidarity
through action.

Protest is the meat and potatoes of the Resistance. Every progressive hero marched. Because it works.

Protestors get the message out to the rest of the populace. A group of people marching in solidarity is impossible to ignore. Gathering in large groups reminds like-minded people that we have strength in numbers, and it also raises awareness on the issues for people who may be on the fence. Protest keeps up morale too. With the day-to-day slog of living under the ridiculous nightmare of having a misogynist, racist, teen-beauty-pageant-locker-room-peeping, conspiracy nut, orange orangutan with a troll-doll-hair comb-over for president is beyond belief, and it can be exhausting! Going to a protest, being there surrounded by fellow patriotic Americans who give a damn about democracy, is inspiring and exhilarating. A protest reminds you that you are not alone. This harrowing era is something we are all going through together.

....

Plutocracy fears protestors because
they are powerful.

....

No single action achieves more than protest. Marching in the streets, holding signs, chanting slogans, it all may seem a little old school in these days of Facebook and Twitter, but the power of words and action in real life will always complete and surpass what the virtual world can do. Protest has always been at the vanguard of real social change. By protest, I mean any type of public gathering that raises awareness, whether it involves a march, a sit-in, or a demonstration. Look at the civil rights era. Everybody remembers Martin Luther King Jr.'s "I Have a Dream" speech, but that speech only makes sense and resonates in the context of the era's protests, sit-ins, boycotts, and marches.

America has a very long history of We the People demanding and getting justice by protest. These movements successfully used marches, rallies, speeches, boycotts, sit-ins, and demonstrations to raise awareness and sway the opinion of the nation at large. Vietnam War protests brought together people from a lot of causes—African American rights, Chicano movements, the clergy, women's liberation, and veterans—all marching for a common, uniting cause. In just a few years, the protests changed how America saw the war, going from 68 percent of Americans agreeing with the war in 1965 down to just 28 percent agreeing with it by 1971.

Now is the time to forge a movement, to forge a unified voice. All the other tactics covered in this book are important too, but probably none more so than protest.

Here is the secret: they say America is a democracy, and everybody gets an equal say in how things are run, but everybody really knows that the game is rigged in favor of the rich and the powerful. The rich can buy influence. The Supreme Court declared with *Citizens United* that corporations giving money to politicians is a form of free speech, which is of course obvious horse-pucky. You don't have to be a lawyer to see through that. It's wrong and unjust.

That is what we are up against. The rich have always used the power of money to keep themselves rich. They may have money on their side, but we have sheer numbers on our side. Ultimately, history has shown that our side, the 99 percent, the Resistance, can be the more powerful side when we get together, when we organize, when we gather, when we march, when we protest. Protest is how we throw our weight around. Protest IS free speech in action.

16.

DONATE

No one has ever become poor by giving.
—Anne Frank

ACTION

Pick a cause that is threatened by the Republican
administration and donate to it.

RESULT

Doing your part to keep the alternative institution of
your choice alive.

One of the first things that the current administration did
was to defund the National Endowment for the Arts. In
the grand scheme of things, when we look at the xenophobia, the
racism, the bigotry of our current leadership, this may not even
seem like that big of a thing—and that really puts into perspective how so very much is under attack. By callously defunding
the NEA, in one fell swoop our government is defunding countless library programs and classes, scholarships and money that
might support struggling playwrights, musicians, artists, as
well as public broadcasting, NPR, access to music lessons, and

programs that bring arts and culture to Americans. Trump is single-handedly decimating museums, the arts, public education, libraries, as well as Big Bird and Bert and Ernie.

There is an old joke: it will be a great day when our schools have all the money they need and the Air Force has to hold a bake sale to buy a bomber. Not only would the world be much more peaceful if we didn't waste half of America's money on killing machines, but that would surely create the most highly trained workforce in the world. Imagine how great that would be for the economy. Even just spending 1 percent of the budget to support national arts would create a new renaissance of historic proportions! (Which would also be great for the economy.) The point I want to make is that you can see the Trump administration is waging war by defunding these things, waging a war against education, against libraries, against the arts and humanities. A war against culture.

Everywhere we look we see areas under threat from the government's agenda. The fact of global warming is dismissed as a hoax, refugees are turned away as Republicans lower immigration limits, environmental protections are rolled away in a bogus pledge to bring coal energy back. Meanwhile the president and his crew set a new low for thinly veiled language that belittles women, African Americans, Latinos, Jews, you name it.

When Puerto Rico was devastated by Hurricane Maria, millions of people were left stranded without electricity, supplies, or clean water, while the Trump administration dragged its heels to lend aid. Trump's excuse was to say Puerto Rico

is "an island surrounded by water. Big Water. Ocean Water."
While the president demonstrated his impressive knowledge of
geography and apparent ignorance of airplanes and boats, the
American people stepped in to donate food, water, batteries,
blankets, diapers, and other much-needed supplies.

Money isn't everything, but when it comes right down to it,
money gets things done. Donating to a cause that you believe
in makes a direct, immediate, positive impact. You can and
should pick the cause that you feel personally drawn to and
contribute to that. Whether you can afford to give a lot or just
a few bucks, charitable causes and organizations need our help
now like never before.

In no particular order, here is list of some great places to
consider donating to.

> Women's health (plannedparenthood.org)
> Global warming (nrdc.org)
> International Refugee Assistance Project
> (refugeerights.org)
> The Trevor Project for LGBTQ youth
> (thetrevorproject.org)
> The Mexican American Legal Defense and Education
> Fund (maldef.org)
> ProPublica, nonprofit journalism (propublica.org)
> Global Fund for Women (globalfundforwomen.org)
> NAACP Legal Defense and Education Fund
> (naacpldf.org)

Wildlife Conservation Society (wcs.org)
Hispanic Scholarship Fund (hsf.net)
American Civil Liberties Union (aclu.org)
National Alliance to End Homelessness
    (endhomelessness.org)
International Peace Institute (ipinst.org)
Oxfam America (oxfam.org)

....

We can fight their greed
with our generosity.

....

17.

VOLUNTEER

You must be the change you wish to see in the world.
—Mahatma Gandhi

ACTION
Volunteer your time.

RESULT
Make the world a better place.

We are at a real turning point for this nation. We will either become stronger, as we work together for compassion, freedom, and equality to overcome this government's evil machinations, or we will be dragged toward a much worse America. I think it is as simple as where people put their time; the side with the most hours will win.

To be a part of the Resistance means to be an activist. To be an activist means to take action. What better way to take action than by volunteering your time for a worthy cause? In a world where many of the problems we see are caused because everything is run for profit, nonprofit organizations bring balance to the picture. There are nonprofits working to feed and clothe the homeless, nonprofits working to provide literacy, education, advocacy, and opportunities to poor children. You can volunteer with programs that teach kids how to play an instrument, or play soccer, or chess, or just be there as a positive role model. There are great programs that provide reading materials to people in jails. There are nonprofits that work to teach yoga to prisoners, nonprofits that train service dogs for war veterans. The possibilities are endless. Sometimes simple is best, and your local churches, soup kitchens, libraries, and after-school programs are likely looking for volunteers right now.

Here are a dozen resources to get you started. With a little research, you'll find many more local groups in your town or city seeking volunteers right now.

- Habitat for Humanity (habitat.org)
- Volunteermatch.org
- Food Not Bombs (foodnotbombs.net)
- Big Brothers Big Sisters of America (bbbs.org)
- Best Buddies (bestbuddies.org)
- United Way (unitedway.org)
- Volunteers of America (voar.org)
- National Audubon Society (audubon.org)
- Raphael House (raphaelhouse.com)

Other places to volunteer include:

- Local libraries
- Food pantries, food banks
- National parks
- Churches
- Shelters
- Neighborhood cleanup days

....

By helping one person at a time,
we make the world a better place.

....

18.

GRAB 'EM BY THE WALLET:
UNIONIZE, STRIKE,
BOYCOTT

Power concedes nothing without a demand.
It never did and it never will.
—Frederick Douglass

ACTION

Boycott Trump and companies that support Trump.

RESULT

Make companies and brands afraid to support
Trump's agenda.

The tactics we are talking about right here are still nonviolent, but they are a bit feistier than some of the other ideas in this book. Strike, unionize, boycott. What do these things have in common? They are about hitting 'em in the wallet. They are tactics that the Left has long used to force the people in power to play fair.

An interesting thing happened while I was writing this chapter—remember when bullshit artist Bill O'Reilly was fired from Fox News, following reports that he had sexually harassed multiple women? The reason that Fox News fired him was because *advertisers* didn't want to be associated with a sexual predator. He wasn't fired because Fox News all of a sudden grew a conscience. Ha ha ha ha! Nope. He was fired because of money.

Just another straightforward example that the thing that matters here is $. It's the only thing that these people really pay attention too. Never underestimate the almighty power of the dollar, and the power of the boycott.

Speaking of sexual predators, Donald Trump's famous boasting that he could just grab women by the pussy (and get away with it because he was "a star"), inspired the Grab Your Wallet boycott movement. This movement was a direct response to the dozen women that came forth and said Donald sexually harassed them, including:

Jessica Leeds—Trump groped her against her will "like an octopus" on an airplane.
Mindy McGillivray—Trump groped her at Mar-a-Lago.
Rachel Crooks—Trump kissed her on the mouth against her will outside an elevator at Trump Tower.
Natasha Stoynoff—Trump physically attacked her, pushed her against a wall, and started "forcing his tongue" down her throat. At Mar-a-Lago.
Temple Taggart—Former Miss USA contestant got the Trump-forced-kiss treatment while in beauty pageant rehearsal. She was twenty-one, he was fifty-one.

Kristin Anderson—Trump did his trademark "grab 'em by the pussy" move on Kristin, touching her at a Manhattan night club against her will.

Cathy Heller—Grabbed and kissed by Trump at Mar-a-Lago.

Summer Zervos—*Apprentice* contestant Trump groped.

Jill Harth—Trump groped under her skirt while making a business deal with her and her boyfriend.

Ivana Trump—Described being raped by Trump.

The list goes on. At least seventeen women came forward publicly, and how many more did not because they didn't want to be attacked by President Trump and his lawyers? These are real people, women with lives, jobs, husbands, kids, families. Trump calls women "pigs," "dogs," and "slobs," and that is how he treats them, as animals to be grabbed.

You can find the boycott list at grabyourwallet.org. This list has gotten results; in response to it, places like Nordstrom and Neiman Marcus have stopped carrying the Trump brand. That's great! Here are the top ten places to boycott for selling Trump junk.

Macy's	Hudson Bay
L.L.Bean	TJ Maxx
Bloomingdale's	Lord & Taylor
Dillard's	Bed Bath & Beyond
Zappos	

Frederick Douglass by Eroyn Franklin

19.

FIGHT RACISM

I refuse to accept the view that mankind is so tragically bound to the starless midnight of racism and war that the bright daybreak of peace and brotherhood can never become a reality . . . I believe that unarmed truth and unconditional love will have the final word.

—Martin Luther King Jr.

ACTION
Take a stand against racism.

RESULT
Be a force for equality.

Racism is alive and well in America. There is a sickening, growing fire of hatred and intolerance that should sound the alarm bell for all good people of all races. We must heal ourselves of this cancer before it kills us.

Racism is an excuse for angry, weak people to try to make themselves feel strong. Racism is a pathetic costume to dress up the cruelty of bullies. The best way to deal with bullies is to stand up to them. It is time for us to talk about racism more openly.

How sad it is that in 2017 we have to redouble our efforts as a

nation to fight against racism. And how disgusting that the catalyst
for this repulsive slide backward is spearheaded by the president!

Growing up in America as a member of a minority I could
look at history and know that while things had been much
worse, in the dark mirror of history, it felt like we as a species
were moving toward a brighter future. There was a hope that
the future might redeem the past.

We should be the country with the greatest racial diversity
and equality in the world. That should be our greatest strength,
and that would be a nation worthy of our patriotism.

We have now witnessed the surreal reality of a clearly bigoted president who loudly defends white supremacists and
neo-Nazis. It is fucking insane. Although it can be hard to pick
which of Trump's crimes against the American people is the
most damaging, I think it is his racism. It undoes so much.

Trump encourages his base to be racist. He said that a judge was
not fit to be an honest judge because he was Mexican. He chose
the CEO of a racist alt-right website, Breitbart, to be his right-hand
man. He attacked the parents of a Muslim US Army officer, with
racist and sexist insinuation. He nominated as attorney general a
guy, Jeff Sessions, who couldn't get nominated as a judge because he
was too racist! Trump said a black protestor was "so obnoxious and
so loud" that "maybe he should be roughed up." His first action as
president was the Muslim ban. Trump thinks he can be as racist as
he wants to be as long as he says he isn't being racist.

This is the battle that will ultimately determine whether the
soul of this nation is permanently disfigured by this president,

or whether we can rise above and grow as a nation by over-coming this man's racist propaganda.

We are being called to heal our culture. We are being called to shut down racist bullies. The place where you live is the place to make a stand. The people that you talk to in your daily life, your coworkers, your family, your friends, are the circle of people your words and actions can influence. Take a conscious stand for racial equality, it begins with setting that intention.

If you are white, take a stand for minorities, not out of guilt but out of pride in the oneness and beauty of the human race. Set an example for other white people. Take action. Speak out for equality not from some sense of white shame for the past but out of the goodness of your heart as a human being. If you are of mixed race, be an ambassador, be a bridge. If you are a minority, be proud of your race and stand up for your rights but also for the rights of others. Speak up for your brothers and sisters of different races. This is so crucial. When Hispanics march for Black Lives Matter, when whites refuse to put up with hearing a racist joke about Asians, when the Asian storefront has a sign in the window that reads "Se Habla Español," when African Americans, Native Americans, Jews, Asian Americans, and transgender people march together in solidarity, that is when we will be too strong to ever be divided and too powerful to be oppressed.

....

Replace racism with humanitarianism,
with internationalism, with peace.

....

Gloria Steinem by Kinoko Evans

20

FIGHT IGNORANCE

*Education is the most powerful weapon which you
can use to change the world.*
—Nelson Mandela

ACTION
Defend and support your local schools, teachers,
colleges, students.

RESULT
Winning the long-term battle of securing the future.

A well-educated public would never have elected Trump in
the first place. A public able to tell the difference between
lies and truth, between fact and fake news, would never have
allowed themselves to be taken in by such openly corrupt politicians. Education is the safeguard of a democracy, because it is
the only thing that gives people the tools they need to defend
themselves from the seductive bullshit of a demagogue.

Education takes work, both from students and teachers, but
also the public at large. I was a high school science teacher, and
I know how much of a struggle it can be to get kids interested

in learning. Sometimes you have to juggle, tap dance, and set something on fire just to keep a classroom's attention. But the thing is, humans like to learn once we overcome that initial laziness. It's fun.

....

Education is the immune
system of democracy.

....

Defending, and strengthening, education is the key to throwing off the shackles of the bullshit artist. That is why Trump picked Betsy DeVos, every public school teacher's worst nightmare, to head the nation's education program. She is also the nightmare of any student who has student loans. She reversed a ban Obama put in place on exorbitantly high fees for defaulted student loans, and she is against student loan for-giveness. DeVos has no experience as an educator, instead she has experience as an anti–public school lobbyist, and being the sibling of Erik Prince, the founder of Blackwater.

This disastrous reality-show administration is built upon a pyramid scheme of lies. That's really all they got. It is essentially the BS of Fox News taken to its logical endpoint. A society that no longer can tell the difference between fact and fiction will always choose the fiction that pleases it the most, no matter how ridiculous and dangerous that fiction is. The antidote is media literacy. The prescription is critical thinking. The cure is a well-funded public education.

How about affordable education, for everybody? From first grade through college. Imagine an America where all public colleges and universities are free. There is no reason that can't be the case. It's absurd that people act like free tuition for college in America is a totally radical idea. College is free in Argentina, Austria, Brazil, the Czech Republic, Denmark, Egypt, Finland, France, Germany, Greece, Iceland, Kenya, Luxembourg, Malaysia, Morocco, Norway, Panama, Poland, Scotland, Slovenia, Spain, Sweden, Turkey, and Uruguay. There is no good reason America shouldn't be on this list.

What we need is a populace of Americans that knows how to read, a population of Americans that knows how to reason, how to think straight, how to understand science, how to read books, write books, how to debate, and how to tell when someone is feeding them a lie. How can anyone disagree with that?

None of this should even be a partisan issue! A nation of smart, critical thinkers should include conservatives and progressives, Democrats and Republicans, traditionalists and Marxists, and socialists, and anarchists, and evangelicals, whatever, every kind of -ism and -ist, all should be allowed to debate, but it should be an educated debate.

Bernie Sanders by Jason McLean

21.

FIGHT INCOME INEQUALITY

*You've got the top 400 Americans owning more wealth than the bottom
150 million Americans. Most folks do not think that is right.*
—Bernie Sanders

ACTION

Fight the growing gap between the super rich and
everyone else.

RESULT

An America that works for everybody.

Technically we live in the richest country in the world, but
most of that money is in the hands of just a few super-rich
people. The gap between the rich and the poor hasn't been this
bad in almost one hundred years. The top one-tenth of 1 percent has more money than the bottom 90 percent of America.
Let that sink in for a minute.

Imagine you are on a boat, or a long bus trip, there are a
hundred people, but one guy hogs as much of everything—the
food, the snacks, the space, air conditioning, etc.—as ninety
other people get. That would be pretty obviously unfair. The

actual situation is much worse than that. The numbers are a bit stupefying at first. You have to give them time to sink in.

Most (58 percent) of all income gains since the Wall Street Crash of 2008 have gone to the top 1 percent wealthiest Americans! No wonder there is more money for a few, but less money for everybody else. This injustice is at the root of all the other problems the country faces.

Hurting Employees

While Trump campaigned with the promise to help the American worker, the actions of his administration once in office have been an all-out attack on blue collar and middle class workers. The Trump administration worked to take away workers' right to bring class action lawsuits against their employers in case of wrongdoing. Trump's picks to his cabinet have been anti-union capitalists, like billionaire Betsy DeVos the secretary of education, and Alexander Acosta the secretary of labor, whose first policy move was to weaken a rule requiring companies to pay employees for overtime.

Labor experts agree one of the most important things for a healthy US job market is innovation and training, but the Trump administration made deep cuts to the labor department, cutting it by 40 percent, as well as cutting funding for job training programs. Trump's labor board, now stocked with people who look out for big business rather than their employees, is currently working to make it harder for employees to form unions.

Trump's labor department has scrapped an Obama-era rule saying that restaurant and bar workers cannot have their tips taken away by the restaurant or bar they work at.

....

Twenty people have as much wealth as half of all Americans.

....

The Senate passed a measure to repeal an Obama-era rule that required companies seeking federal contracts to disclose violations of labor standards like safety and fair pay rules. The Trump labor department has been targeting the Occupational Safety and Health Administration (OSHA) and hamstringing the agency's ability to look after the safety and health of workers in a variety of ways. For example, they have drastically reduced the time in which companies are required to report accidents happening on the job, effectively making the reporting of safety violations voluntary. The labor department also is no longer making records public when companies violate health and safety standards. This sends a signal to CEOs and business owners that they can treat their employers however they like because nobody in this administration is really looking out for the workers.

Trump's labor department is seeking to eliminate the Federal Employees Retirement System for all new government hires. These same White House officials are planning a wage freeze for federal employees in 2019 and taking away paid holidays for federal employees, according to leaked documents. While the administration smiles and pretends to embrace the worker, really it is so they can stick a knife in the worker's back.

There are very practical tactics and policies that can combat this.

- Fairly tax big corporations, so they pay their fair share.
- Tax Wall Street.
- Progressive tax on millionaires.
- Raise the minimum wage.
- Work on pay equity so that woman earn the same dollar, per dollar, for doing the same jobs as men do.
- Make it easier for people to unionize.
- Break up the big banks!

When the wealth gap has gotten as crazy out of control as it is, all of this should just be seen as common sense. The reason it isn't has a lot to do with the super rich using their money to control and manage public opinion, and to paint these common-sense ideas as radical, when they are really anything but!

The truth of the matter is that the American dream has been withering on the vine for some time. More and more you hear about kids these days who can't afford to move out of their parents' house. I assure you it is not because this generation is lazier than previous generations. When I hang out with my buddies and we talk politics, we always laugh when the news says the economy is doing well, because it sure isn't going up for most of us, who are working menial jobs to get by. Opportunity in the land of opportunity has been drying up. People are so sick of not getting their fair shot at the American dream that a lot of them were bitter enough to be willing to be swindled by a huckster. We can find a better way.

The world is the way it is because people have made it so. There is no reason we can't fix the widening wealth gap if we choose to do so. We can fix this, not only because it is the right thing to do, but also because it is a winning strategy politically.

22.

PROTECT THE
ENVIRONMENT

*A nation that destroys its soils destroys itself. Forests are the lungs of our
land, purifying the air and giving fresh strength to our people.*
—Franklin D. Roosevelt

ACTION
Prioritize protecting the environment.

RESULT
An inhabitable planet for future generations.

In reneging on America's commitment to the Paris climate
accord, Trump walked away from the planet's best hope of
fighting global warming. Earth will continue to get hotter and sea
levels will continue to rise, so that oil companies can continue to
make money at the expense of the earth's future. However, Trump
pulling out of the Paris climate accord is also an example of how
Americans can defy him and still do the right thing. Three hundred mayors and a dozen states have committed to continuing to
combat climate change regardless of the country's overall drift.

The EPA

Of course it is not just Trump. As we have seen across the board, much of the harm being done is caused by this administration's cabinet members, and agency chiefs, and Republican-controlled Congress. Trump's pick to head the EPA, Scott Pruitt, is a grievous example of the damage being done by stocking this administration with corporate stooges as Trump has done. They in turn fill the positions of bureaucracy beneath them with yet more corporate stooges and industry insiders, all the way down the line. Trump directed Pruitt to cut the EPA budget 40 percent, and roll back regulations on clean water protection and climate change prevention. Pruitt has worked to destroy everything the EPA has stood for and is turning it into a force that caters exclusively to business interests. Under Pruitt, a former lawyer who spent his career as an aggressive adversary of the environment—suing the EPA fourteen times in order to allow more pollution—the agency has halted its work to fight global warming and instead is moving to deregulate coal, power plants, oil, and pollution.

To put it bluntly, these swine want to poison the water and overheat the earth for money. Pruitt barred scientists in academia from being on the EPA board, instead filling it with industry insiders. To head the science advisory board, Pruitt installed a quack named Honeycutt, a Texas toxicologist who has spent his entire career arguing against every protection the EPA has ever put in place to help people; this is a guy who says pollution "isn't that bad for people." Honeycutt also said ozone standards made "no biological sense" because "most people spend more than 90% of their time indoors." Yes, that is a real quote from the person currently advising the EPA on pollution.

With these kinds of people in charge, terrible and lasting

....

> How much better it is to choose to
> be on the side fighting for nature!

....

damage is being done: the EPA is dismantling its Clean Power plan, the administration is green-lighting the Dakota Access Pipeline and the Keystone XL Pipeline, thousands of acres of national monuments have been sold off to oil companies, the Arctic and Atlantic oceans have been opened for more offshore drilling, and the EPA has canceled limits on the pollutants power plants can dump into water, so they can get away with dumping aluminum, arsenic, and mercury into streams, rivers, and lakes. They have replaced the very agency meant to protect the air with people who want to pollute the air to make cash for rich corporations.

What is frightening is that despite—or because of—the sheer volume of assaults this administration has launched upon the regulations put in place to protect animals and nature, much of it goes unnoticed. Consider the fate of the Pacific walrus. These beautiful animals are dying off because they cannot adapt to the rising temperatures of climate change, but the current administration has blocked a move to put them on the endangered species list. This walrus depends upon shelves of Arctic summer ice to breed and raise its young; at current rates, that ice will have melted away completely by 2030. Scientists have stated the administration's move to block placing them on the endangered list is "a death sentence." Sadly, the awareness of the plight of endangered animals must now be raised by people outside of the government. To quote Brett Hartl, a director at the Center for Biological Diversity, "Republicans in Congress continue to attack the Endangered Species Act despite overwhelming support from Americans of all political stripes . . . These attacks are designed to reward special interests that would plunder our natural resources even if it causes wildlife to go extinct."

The clock is ticking. If Trump is kicked out of office by 2020, we can opt to stay in the Paris climate accord. That would be a wonderful first step toward doing what must be done to literally save the planet.

Save the Environment Now Not Tomorrow

As I write, Texas is being devastated by flooding and hurricanes. The forests of the West Coast are suffering massive fires as temperatures continue to rise.

In Portland, Oregon, where I live, for days the sky was darkened by smoke from nearby forest fires, the air was thick and hard to breathe. I've worked as a forest firefighter, but to see this happening from my own front yard really brought home just how immediate all of this is. For days the sun was blood red and daylight was a haunted gray dusk. People came down with headaches and dry coughs as the sky rained down flakes of ash and soot, covering cars and sidewalks with a hellish version of snow. It feels apocalyptic because it is. The destruction of our world is happening right now before our very eyes. The fate of the world depends upon the battle between those who can see the truth and speak up for it, and those who want society to turn a blind eye to the damage that we as a species are doing to our planet.

Vaclav Havel by Robert Dayton

23.

SAMIZDAT: GET THE MESSAGE OUT

A modern revolutionary group heads for the television station.
—Abbie Hoffman

ACTION

Get the message out.

RESULT

Raising awareness by informing your friends and
community of what is going on and what they
can do about it.

In Soviet Russia, written dissent was suppressed brutally. Any writing that the government didn't like was banned, and the authors could be thrown in jail. In response to this, people would still communicate the uncensored truth, but they had to do so by going underground. *Samizdat*—pamphlets that were written, published, and spread in secret, and at great risk—were the only way that people could express what they truly believed. The example of samizdat demonstrates that everyday people, using simple methods, can fight censorship and refuse to be silenced.

Right now we have access to an incredible variety of ways we can make our voice heard, and it is vital that we do so. It is by spreading the message of resistance, why it matters and what we can do, that we take a stand for the truth and thereby win over hearts and minds.

Signs

Signs, graffiti, bumper stickers, it all counts. Do not under-estimate the impact that a message can have when it is repeated in everyday places, on a billboard, scrawled on a wall, a bumper, a lapel button. The zeitgeist grows ubiquitous by being visible.

Symbols

Throughout history, bullies have always understood the power of the symbol. Trump-land certainly understands that symbols have power, as did the Nazis. This is a war of ideas, but also a battle of symbols. Be perceptive to symbols of resistance. Create and propagate new symbols. Symbols are free to evolve, they are not static. It is time for new symbols of resistance.

Public Speaking

Free speech at its most essential can mean talking to a small group of friends or a crowd and sharing what you believe. Standing up and delivering an extemporaneous speech that stirs up a crowd is certainly not for everyone, but consider the impact of your day-to-day interactions and conversations. There is the kind of censorship where speaking out against the government is illegal, but there is another more subtle and insidious form of censorship where people censor themselves from saying what they know to be true for fear of rocking the boat. Beware of both.

Art

Art can be profound, sublime, mysterious, and sacred. There is no damn reason it can't also be about the very practical issues that we as human beings on this planet are up against right now, and do so in an inspiring, meaningful way. Make art that speaks to what is going on in the world, not merely art as an escape. Poems, essays, stories, plays, paintings, images, photography, songs—all art can be a part of an incredibly powerful voice to help get the message of resistance out.

Zines

Zines cost next to nothing to make, and are easy to distribute. They require nothing more than a copy machine and a stapler. They are the ultimate underground messaging system. Truth desires to be free.

Radio

Guerrilla radio stations may not be quite as hard to set up as you might think. You need a microphone and a transmitter. And ideally a comfortable enough place you can spend time in broadcasting. Anybody can get one going with just a garage and a few hundred to a few thousand bucks. This is more of a group project than an individual one, therefore if you already have access to independent radio, support it!

Podcasts

It is easier than ever to broadcast ideas to listeners anywhere in the world with podcasts. I've made podcasts sitting on my friend's couch and sharing a six-pack. It's low budget and easy to do. You need a microphone and a recording device such as a laptop, that's it.

Blogs

Anyone can start a blog, publish their voice, and make their ideas available to everyone; and it's free to set up. Think of it as the modern, digital equivalent of the zine.

....

Raise your voice!

....

24.

TRUMP-RUSSIA: CONNECT THE DOTS

Watergate pales really in my view compared to what we're confronting now. I am very concerned about the assault on our institutions coming from both an external source—read Russia— and an internal source, the president himself.
—James Clapper, former director of National Intelligence

ACTION

Understand the known evidence of Trump-Russia collusion and add to it as more comes to light.

RESULT

A deep conviction that this president must be impeached.

Here is a timeline consisting of basic facts that we know about Trump's campaign and Russia. Keep in mind this is the tip of the iceberg.

#1. Trump's connections to Russia go way back

After several bankruptcies in the 1990s, American banks

stopped loaning Trump money. He was bailed out by loans from Russian financiers with ties to Putin. In 2008, Don Jr. told investors that "a disproportionate percentage" of the Trump Organization's money comes from Russia. Breaking with decades of tradition, Trump was the first presidential candidate to refuse to release his tax returns. The Steele Dossier alleges that Putin had been "cultivating" Trump for years and the Kremlin has a kompromat videotape of Donald Trump paying Moscow prostitutes to pee on a bed.

#2. Trump campaign aide Papadopoulos established a Trump-Putin back channel

March 2016: Papadopoulos traveled to meet with a Russian who had promised dirt on Clinton in the form of e-mails. Papadopoulos later pled guilty to lying to the FBI about that conversation. Papadopoulos told Trump at a face-to-face meeting that he was an intermediary working to establish a Trump-Putin back channel. Trump expressed interest. In May 2016 Papadopoulos drunkenly bragged to an Australian diplomat that Russia had acquired political dirt on Clinton.

#3. Russia hacked the 2016 election

March 2016: Russia gained access to Clinton campaign chairman John Podesta's e-mails which they "weaponized" by releasing to WikiLeaks. The CIA, NSA, and FBI agree this was part of a coordinated effort by Russia to help Trump win the election. Russia also targeted the voting databases of twenty-one states, gaining access to voters' personal information, and targeted American voters with pro-Trump ads on Facebook reaching 126 million people, half the total US voting population.

#4. Trump's campaign was staffed with Russophiles

May 19, 2016: Paul Manafort became Trump's campaign manager. His previous experience had been working for the Russian-backed ex-president of the Ukraine. Manafort offered Oleg Deripaska, a Russian billionaire close to the Kremlin, "private briefings" on the Trump campaign. Michael Flynn joined the Trump campaign as its first major foreign policy adviser. In 2015, the Russian government paid Flynn $45,000 to attend a Kremlin gala and sit next to Putin.

#5. Don Jr. met with Russians to get dirt on Clinton

June 3, 2016: When Don Jr. received an e-mail from the Russians offering illegally obtained dirt on Clinton, he responded "if it's what you say I love it." He set up a meeting to obtain the offered information. Trump Jr., Manafort, and Kushner all attended the meeting, which shows how seriously the campaign was taking the offer of Russian help in contaminating the election.

#6. Carter Page went to Moscow to discuss lifting sanctions against Russia

July 7, 2016: Carter Page, a Trump foreign policy adviser with experience working in the Moscow oil industry, flies to Russia for a meeting. At first he claimed this was for an academic meeting, however his story later changed to include meeting with Russian state officials and high-ranking members of Rosneft, the Russian oil company. The Steele Dossier alleges he met with the Rosneft CEO to be offered a slice of the profits from a huge Rosneft sale if Trump lifted sanctions.

#7. Trump changed the language of the Republican platform to be pro-Russia

Trump changed the language of the Republican Party platform to be pro-Russia: getting rid of language that endorsed providing arms to Ukraine's government in its fight against being taken over by Russia. When asked about this change, Trump lied and said it never happened. At Trump's first major foreign policy speech, he invited Russian agent Sergey Kislyak to sit in the front row as he promised Russia "a good deal" on sanctions.

#8. Sessions met with a Russian ambassador, then lied about it under oath

July 18, 2016: Jeff Sessions met with Kislyak and discussed Trump's campaign and presidential policy issues with the Russian ambassador before the election, multiple times. Sessions later lied about this and other Russian contacts, both verbally and in writing, under oath to Congress. US intelligence officials have described Kislyak as a top Russian spy and a recruiter of spies. This is, as they say, *not normal.*

#9. Trump asked Russia to hack Clinton's e-mails

July 27, 2016: At the last press conference of his campaign, Trump said on national TV, "Russia, if you're listening, I hope you're able to find the thirty thousand e-mails that are missing." Trump encouraged a foreign power to meddle in our election, strong evidence that he was aware of the Russian hacking before the e-mails were released.

#10. WikiLeaks publishes first e-mails provided by Russia

July 22, 2016: Russian hackers gained access to John Podesta's e-mails as well as e-mails from the DNC server. These became the centerpiece of an ongoing campaign by Russia to "weaponize" the e-mails, releasing them to WikiLeaks and damaging the Clinton campaign in order to help Trump win the election.

#11. Manafort was discovered to have been secretly paid $12.7 million by the Russian-backed Ukraine president

August 19, 2016: Trump's campaign manager had a long history of pro-Russia ties. Manafort and Trump had known each other since the '80s. Manafort was indicted for working secretly as a foreign agent and then laundering tens of millions of dollars in order to not pay taxes.

#12. Roger Stone knew about Podesta e-mails before anyone else

August 21, 2016: Before any of the e-mails Russia had stolen from Clinton's campaign chair were released, Stone, an informal

Trump campaign adviser, tweeted that it "will soon be Podesta's time in the barrel."

#13. Jeff Sessions secretly met (again) with the Russian ambassador behind closed doors

September 2016: Sessions had a private meeting with Sergey Kislyak in his own office behind closed doors, at the height of what US intelligence officials say was a Russian cyber campaign to hack the US presidential election. He later lied about this conversation under oath during his confirmation hearing to become attorney general.

#14. Jared Kushner proposed a secret back channel with Russians

December 2016: Less than a month after the election, Kushner and Flynn sneak Kislyak into Trump Tower to discuss the creation of a secret backdoor line of communication. Kushner suggested to Kislyak a clandestine back channel between Trump and Russia. Given that America and Russia already have open lines of communication, the only purpose of a back channel would be to avoid monitoring by American intelligence. Kushner and Flynn don't disclose this meeting with a hostile foreign power, which constitutes espionage.

#15. Flynn called the Russian ambassador to discuss lifting sanctions

After President Obama placed sanctions on Russia for the cyber attack on the presidential election, Flynn, with full knowledge of Trump's transition team, conducted illegal discussions with Russia on lifting sanctions. Flynn made phone calls to the Russians to reassure them that Trump would lift sanctions against Russia. When asked about these conversations by the FBI he lied. When acting attorney general Yates warned Trump that Flynn—his national security adviser—had been compromised by Russia, Trump fired her and kept Flynn on board for eighteen days. Flynn has since pled guilty.

#16. Sessions lied about Kislyak meetings

During his senate hearing, Sessions insisted he had no contact with Russian agents; when evidence proved this a lie he recused himself from the ongoing investigation into Russia. Sessions no longer being able to steer the investigation into Russia infuriated Trump.

#17. President Trump revealed plans to drop all sanctions on Russia

Ex-mobster and Trump crony Felix Sater and Trump's lawyer Michael Cohen snuck a Kremlin-approved "peace deal" to Flynn. All involved lied about their actions. Days after taking office, Trump revealed a plan to drop all sanctions against Russia despite their unprecedented cyber attack on the American presidential election. Officials were shocked that Trump was going to give the Russians exactly what they wanted.

#18. Trump dictated a cover story for Don Jr. about the "Russian adoption"

When it was revealed that Don Jr. was seeking illegally obtained "dirt" in meeting with the Russians, Donald Trump personally dictated the cover story that they were meeting to discuss "the adoption of Russian children." One does not fabricate a lie except to hide the truth.

#19. Trump fired Comey because of Russia

Trump invited Comey to a private dinner where he asked the FBI director to pledge his loyalty to Trump personally. Later Trump had a meeting where he asked everyone to leave the room so he could ask James Comey to stop investigating Flynn. When Comey would not cooperate with Trump's obstruction of justice, Trump fired him. At first he lied about why he did this but soon admitted on national TV that he fired Comey due to "the Russia thing." He also gloated in a private meeting with Russian agents—where no American press was allowed—that he had fired Comey to stop him from investigating Trump's connections to Russia.

Any one of these points would be evidence of collusion between the Trump campaign and Russia. Considered together, they paint a damning narrative of active collusion. The odds that George Papadopoulos, Manafort, Flynn, Donald Jr., Jeff Sessions, Roger Stone, Carter Page, and Jared Kushner acted to collude with Russia without informing the person they were advising and working for are nil.

The only picture that explains the known facts is Trump and his administration actively worked with Russia, in collusion, to hack the American election. Trump made a deal to lift American sanctions on Russia in exchange for Russia's help winning the election. Since becoming president, Trump has lied and obstructed justice to prevent the truth from coming to light.

25.

IGNORE
DISTRACTIONS

ACTION
Stay focused.

RESULT
You'll know what's true and what isn't.

Trump is a television creature, a weak man's idea of a strong man, a poor person's idea of rich. His whole shtick is just showbiz—don't look behind the curtain and we will put on a show!

Even the never-ending leaks and revelations surrounding the Russia scandal distract us from agenda items like gutting health care and environmental regulations and giving tax cuts to the wealthy. The tweets, the outrage, the ongoing carnival atmosphere, that's all part of the distraction.

We live in a new world where politics have become binge TV. The president's lies have never been very good or convincing, but they don't need to be.

Our president lies as easily as he breathes. Don't forget that you are dealing with a man who built a fake university to defraud poor suckers seeking an education. Eventually every con artist is unmasked. Stay cool and calm. Stick to the facts.

26.

HOPE FOR THE BEST, BE PREPARED FOR THE WORST

We must accept finite disappointment, but never lose infinite hope.
—Martin Luther King Jr.

ACTION

Take a moment to imagine just how bad things
will get under Trump's rule. Also, make sure
your passport is up to date.

RESULT

A better understanding of what we are fighting for
and what we are fighting against.

To fully understand why it is important that we resist, we
must imagine what will happen if we do not.

2017

In hindsight, maybe historians will say everything that came
after the firing of James Comey was inevitable. The signs were
all there. It started with unchecked lies and attacking the
freedom of the press. However, we were told to look on the

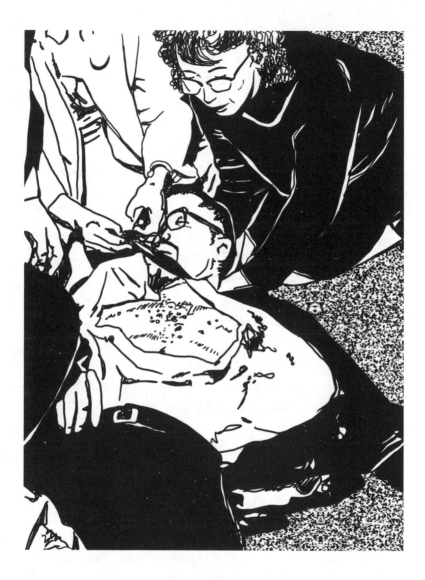

Yuri Kochiyama by Alex Chiu

bright side—after all, tax cuts for the wealthy would surely trickle down to create jobs for the rest of us.

2018

Everything is fine. The president tweets some new outrageous lie or Breitbart conspiracy on a weekly basis, and some news organizations still fact-check him, but there have been no real consequences, and people are too tired to care anymore.

Maybe you can take up bird-watching or growing tomatoes. It's good to have some distraction, because even little glimpses of the truth are scary.

2019

The wall with Mexico has cost taxpayers close to $25 billion; it is unfinished. Trump still promises that Mexico will pay for it. The Trump administration has stepped up its raids on sanctuary cities, with militarily armed ICE agents arresting millions of men, women, and children and taking them to concentration camps from where they are deported. Trump is proud of the jobs these "detention centers" create. Environmental regulations have been rolled back to levels no one has imagined since the 1950s. The national parks are sold to the highest bidder, privatized, and opened for drilling. Pollution in cities and on shorelines is rampant. Entire forests and bodies of water are sold off for profit.

White nationalist militia groups have escalated their violence. They have flags and names that include the words "freedom" and "eagles." They "assist" the local police.

The congressional investigation into Trump's Russian ties, now led by Trump's own handpicked men, announces that Trump did "nothing wrong," and people should move on. Trump and DeVos legislate billions of dollars away from public schools. Education is a product, like cell phones and Coca-Cola.

Encouraged by the new normal, outright racism has made a comeback to 1950s levels. Alt-right leaders openly begin to talk about "peaceful ethnic cleansing." Trump seems to support the idea in a tweet.

2020

The ice caps are melting faster every day. Temperatures rise faster than predicted, massive wildfires and huge hurricanes are commonplace. Jokes about the apocalypse no longer get laughs. And yet people continue to disbelieve everything that is actually happening because it is too awful to fully believe.

When a terrorist attack happens just before the election it could not have been scripted at a better time by Steve Bannon himself. Future historians will argue for decades about what started the war. A year into the war, most Americans will struggle to correctly remember how it started. Patriotism will be at an all-time high. Trump wins reelection, easily beating the moderate Democratic candidate.

2021

It turns out that, yes, Trump does keep a very long enemies list. Rabble-rousers, protestors, and many journalists are jailed for treason. Some are "reeducated." Some disappear mysteriously. Some flee. There are rumors of waterboarding, but who is to say? In a world that is post-fact and post-truth, the idea of right and wrong sounds quaint. Like many people, you decide it is smart and safe to keep quiet. People who do criticize the government put their phones in sealed plastic baggies in the freezer first.

....
The folks that make up the Republican
base are being played for suckers.
....

2022

The consequences of electing a president who sexually harassed dozens of women and bragged about it on videotape are confirmed. There has been a cultural shift in society's attitudes toward women. The idea of feminism is seen as a strange historic aberration that lives on only in textbooks.

Muslims begin to worship in secret for safety reasons. It is not a good year to be Latinx. It is no longer illegal to discriminate. It starts with Mexicans and Muslims. Trump supporters praise the new culture, the freedom finally from political correctness. Now everyone can act and talk like Trump. This works out quite well for white men especially. This is also the year that they make it illegal to vote unless you own property. There are more parades.

2023

Some days the sky is an ominous color. Is that something burning in the distance? Don't bother reading the news. Facts aren't distinguished from fiction at this point anyhow. The government can now experiment with brutality in the name of safety. People are more afraid than ever, but Trump will protect them, with walls, with prisons, with camps called "centers," with a robust domestic surveillance program called "Vigilant something-or-other" and with enhanced interrogations performed by "truth agents," and black sites where treasonous enemies of the state disappear. Language has become murky and poisonous.

2024

To own a book like the one in your hands is to risk being jailed for treason. Looking back, you may secretly wonder when did we reach the turning point when this all became inevitable, the point of no return?

The 2024 presidential election was canceled due to special emergency circumstances. Congress voted unanimously. It always does now. Trump declares a huge day of celebration. There are rallies and pageantry that would make Kim Jong-il jealous. Incredibly large statues are in the works. It is a magnificent spectacle, this reality show on steroids, with tweets, rallies, and banners. Yes, bringing up Hitler is always in poor taste. Finally, America is great again.

27.

FIGHT FOR THE TRUTH

Darkness cannot drive out darkness; only light can do that. Hate cannot drive out hate; only love can do that.
—Martin Luther King Jr.

ACTION
Call Trump on his BS.

RESULT
A refusal to surrender the truth.

Trump lied about Obama wiretapping Trump Tower. He lied about taping his conversations with Comey and about the size of his inauguration crowds. He even lied about making a typo on Twitter, misspelling news coverage as news "covfefe," and then had the chutzpah to lie and pretend he did this on purpose. What a jackass! In the words of Obama, "he's nothing but a bullshitter."

The technical term for "bullshitter" is "pathological liar." This is a symptom of people who are narcissistic. A breakdown of narcissistic personality disorder reads like a quick summary of Trump's most salient personality traits.

Dorothy Day by Liz Yerby

- Exaggerated feelings of self-importance
- Needing constant admiration from others
- Lack of understanding for others' feelings
- Exploitative of others for personal gain
- Pompous and arrogant
- Secretly prone to feelings of humiliation and worthlessness over minor incidents

The term "con artist" comes from "confidence man." A confidence man works by first gaining people's confidence in order to rip them off, like Trump did with his bogus university, and like he is doing now—in running a criminal enterprise from the White House.

From lying about Obama's birth certificate, to lying about the size of his inauguration crowd, to lying about "3 million illegal voters," there are too many lies to track them all, but being aware of the size and frequency of his pathological lying will prevent you from becoming acclimated to the lies.

Facebook & Fake News

It has become increasingly clear that Facebook played a pivotal role in helping Trump to win the election. Facebook was flooded with fake news—this weak spot in our media was used by the Russians, who paid for advertising on Facebook that was pro-Trump and anti-Clinton. Obviously the rules for advertising on social media also need to be shored up to prevent this kind of foreign meddling.

We need to demand changes to our social media platforms. Fake news is created to generate clicks on websites that sell advertising. Take away the financial incentive and fake news would die. Websites that purport to be factual news should be subject to third-party fact-checkers that can alert people when the "news" they have clicked on is just a bunch of BS. We demanded that the food industry started using labels to let people know what is in the food they eat.

....

Don't be a victim to gaslighting.

....

28.

FIND YOUR PASSION,
DO YOUR THING

*The key to organizing an alternative society is to organize
people around what they can do, and more importantly,
what they want to do.*
—Abbie Hoffman

ACTION
Don't try to do everything, instead
identify your passion.

RESULT
Focus. Make a real difference in one area.

I play chess. One of the first lessons you learn in chess is that a good strategy is one that can adapt to changing circumstances. If you focus on one objective and don't pay attention to what your opponent is up to, they will always be a few steps ahead of you. In the Resistance we should think strategically, like chess players; that means paying attention to what our opponent is doing and reacting accordingly. Wherever they focus their agenda, the Resistance is there applying pressure

Nina Simone by Theo Ellsworth

too, fighting back, reducing the damage they can do, politically and culturally. This is an ongoing battle where it pays to look at the big picture, as well as what is happening in the moment.

Or think of it like a soccer game. Contrary to our natural impulse to just run toward wherever the action is, it is much more efficient and effective for people to get really good at their specific positions, to play a role supporting the team.

Finding your position on Team Resistance means striking the right balance between being able to shift with the upcoming twists and turns and sticking to the thing that you are most passionate about. Let's say you are someone who feels called to take a stand for the environment; that's great, and you can focus your efforts fighting the Trump administration's efforts to roll back laws that protect our national parks and the oceans, allowing oil companies to drill for oil where they will do real damage to the environment. You are doing your part. It's still necessary to keep your eye on the overall battle, but stick to your position.

You should pick the battle that speaks to you personally. If for you that means fighting back against wealth inequality, or racism, or if that is working on the front lines of protests— whatever it is that speaks to you, that is the role that you should embrace, fully and completely. No one should feel bad they don't have time to be an expert on every single issue!

You are part of the resistance. We should not lose sight of the fact that we are all on the same side, from the person marching in the street with a sign, to those politicians who speak out against Trump, to the journalist or publisher bringing a steady flow of information to the reading public. When a nation finds its voice, it is a truly beautiful thing to behold.

PART 3
LIBERATE!

29.
IMPEACH THE PRESIDENT

When the government fears the people, there is liberty. When the people
fear the government, there is tyranny.
—Thomas Jefferson

ACTION

Impeach the president.

RESULT

Get Trump out of office while our
democracy is still intact.

There is a race between how fast we can get this demagogue out of office and how much damage he can do In
the meantime. The longer he remains in office, the faster he
dismantles the "checks and balances" that were put in place
to prevent a creature such as himself from taking over. Make
no mistake, Trump threatening to jail journalists and firing the
FBI director were clear shots fired in an ongoing war between
autocracy and democracy.

The possibility of someone like Donald reaching the White
House is the very reason impeachment was invented. Even if

Congress tries to impeach Trump and fails to pull it off completely, the process of impeachment would leave him badly damaged, and that, dear reader, would be a sweet and lovely thing.

So how does impeachment work? The power to impeach a president is written into the Constitution, as a power of Congress. Keep in mind, Congress will behave according to what its members think will get them reelected. Therefore, We the People should pressure Congress for impeachment in order to make it happen. Impeachment starts in the House of Representatives. It works much like a bill moving through Congress (except the president cannot veto it!). First, the House of Representatives votes on whether there are grounds for impeachment. If yes, it then moves on to the Senate, where it would need two-thirds of the Senate, sixty-seven aye votes, for impeachment to happen, at which point Trump would be removed from office and could be indicted for his crimes.

The closest any president has ever come to being impeached and removed was Richard Nixon in 1974. Nixon resigned the day before the big vote because he saw the writing on the wall. Watergate involved a break-in of the DNC; the stuff Trump appears to be involved in makes Watergate look like small potatoes by comparison. The Constitution specifically states impeachable offenses as "Treason, Bribery, or other high Crimes and Misdemeanors."

Treason

Russia wanted Trump to win the election. Colluding with Russia to hack the American election is about as treasonous an act as we can imagine. Trump's campaign contacted Russia secretly during the run-up to the election, and then lied about it countless times.

Bribery

The Constitution states that a person in office cannot accept "emoluments" (presents, money) from foreign powers. The reason for this is obvious, to prevent people like the president from being bribed with gifts and money. Trump is bribed on the regular by foreign powers through his hotels and businesses. Visiting diplomats pay to stay in Trump luxury hotels. This is exactly the thing the framers of the Constitution were trying to prevent, which is why they made it illegal. One cannot be president of the United States and owner of a global business empire like Trump's at the same time.

High Crimes and Misdemeanors

Obstruction of justice is an impeachable high crime. Trump committed obstruction of justice by ham-fistedly pressuring FBI director James Comey to drop the investigation into Russia. You know the story—Trump made sure to pressure Comey to drop his investigation privately, which shows he knew what he was doing was illegal. When Comey did not drop the Russia investigation, Trump fired him. Trump even went on national

TV and confessed that he fired Comey because of Russia. This is clear-cut, unambiguous obstruction of justice.

We already have plenty of well-defined legal justifications to impeach Trump. What we need now is enough Democrats in Congress, as well as Republicans willing to put country ahead of party, to get the votes to do the right thing. Therefore, the first step to impeach really begins with giving Democrats the control of the House. Remember this during the midterm elections, and do everything you can to help out with local and state elections—winning control of the House is the first step to impeaching Trump.

30

ONCE UPON A TIME

The future is unwritten.

—Joe Strummer

ACTION

Imagine an ending to this fairy tale.

RESULT

The future is unwritten, and therefore it is
up to us to write it.

Once upon a time . . . there was a prosperous kingdom. It was large, with plenty of elbow room, a land of many different types of people, elves, druids, centaurs, mermaids, and so on, vast and beautiful, with flowing rivers, snow-capped mountains, ample beaches, deserts, and enchanting forests.

Now it so happened that in this kingdom there was a slimy and foul toad. This mean little toad was selfish, stupid, and a natural-born liar. It was the kind of toad that normally would only be talked about by parents telling their children scary stories of what kind of person not to be. The toad was racist toward hobbits and elves. It boasted of grabbing damsels against their will. Everybody chuckled about this toad, because it went around bragging all the time that it was a beautiful prince, a wise sage, and an excellent knight—when it was quite plain for all to see it was just a lumpy, fat, old toad.

One day, however, this toad came upon a witch, who was visiting the swamp to gather some eye of newt. This witch enjoyed mayhem and mischief. The witch knew she had found something truly rare in this puffed-up and conceited little toad.

"You know, my stinky little creature, I have a magic spell that works upon the vanity of anyone, creating an illusion so that others will believe it too. With this charm, you can mesmerize almost half the kingdom."

And so the witch taught the toad a spell, which was actually the ugly croaking sound of "ME! ME! ME!"

Those who fell under this spell would believe the toad when he claimed to be a wise, handsome, and noble prince.

Down the road that toad hopped, croaking, "ME! ME! ME!"

The toad came to a village, where the villagers were out farming in the fields.

The toad hopped into the center of the town square and began to puff itself up and croak his magic spell: "ME! ME! ME!"

The dark magic worked like this: it magnified fear and hate, and distrust, and selfishness, taking root in people's hearts.

Soon the toad had the villagers all worked up. The villagers were scared of all sorts of fantastical, extremely rare creatures and phenomena. The usual stuff: evil wizards, leprechauns, ogres, goblins.

The magical spell only worked on about one out four people who heard it, but this turned out to be enough. Many other people just went along with it.

The toad croaked to his followers, "I am the smartest, the fanciest toad! Uh, I mean, mighty ogre! And this country is under attack! From all kinds of bad things! Boogeymen and unicorns and scary salamanders! Only I can save you!

"You just have to follow me to the castle and make me king!"

And so the toad marched with his band of followers, wearing a little crown it had fashioned from a soup can. Of course, many people just laughed. They thought it was all a joke. As the toad's parade marched across the kingdom, many people joined it when they heard it was being lead by a mighty ogre who promised to keep them safe.

Some rich merchants and bankers saw what was happening. This was plainly a toad that had somehow fooled a lot of villagers into thinking it was a powerful ogre. The fat merchants and bankers told each other, let's just go along with it, and hopefully the toad will lower our taxes. And so they welcomed the toad in through the palace gates.

That was how the toad actually became king. Immediately he began issuing royal decrees. The toad made it illegal for certain races to enter the country. The toad had all the candle-stick makers banished, and sent overseas or to jail (the toad said this was to prevent forest fires). And of course, since this is just a medieval fairy tale and not real life, the toad had a gigantic wall built along the border of the whole country to keep out invaders, who might try to sneak in to help work on the farms.

The court advisers were dumbfounded at first.

"What should we do? This new toad, er, I mean, king ogre, is obviously out of his mind! His royal decrees make no sense!"

By now rumors were everywhere that the king ogre was just a toad who had been hexed by the kingdom's sworn enemy, the evil witch. People who said this out loud where accused of heresy and locked up in the stockades.

The richest, fattest merchant spoke up first, "The toad has no idea how to be king! It's a toad, after all. So, we can get all of our schemes that we have long dreamed of. Tax cuts for ourselves, to be specific. What else is there to care about, really? As long as nobody uncovers the truth about the witch and the fact that he is just a dumb toad, what could possibly go wrong?"

"Hear hear!"

"It is agreed! We must pretend that every crazy thing the toad says is reasonable and beautiful."

And so that is what they did.

······································

A toad with a crown is still a toad.

······································

31.

FACE YOUR SHADOW

In the practice of tolerance, one's enemy is the best teacher.
—the Dalai Lama

ACTION

Face your shadow.

RESULT

Steal the secret source of the
shadow's power—denial.

Here is what Trump is. He is the part of the nation, the part of ourselves, that we wish wasn't there. He is vain. He is dumb. He is illiterate. He mocked a disabled man's disability in front of a crowd of thousands. He is vulgar. He boasted of sexually assaulting women. He is racist. He makes fun of veterans and cripples. He makes fun of fat people. He makes fun of women. He calls everyone a loser. He is filled with spite, and ugly as the bottom of an outhouse, but he clucks and squawks around like a vain old rooster. He has no shame. That is the secret to his success. Trump is our nation's shadow. He is the worst part of ourselves.

Abraham Lincoln by Ben Heiken

He is the shadow of the red and the blue states. Not just the red states. That is important to own up to. In a way, we have created him together. He is the zeitgeist of America.

What I'm trying to hip you to is Swiss psychologist Carl Jung's theories about human nature. He had this theory that humans have a shadow self. The shadow is basically the part of oneself that is embarrassing or shameful.

Everybody has a shadow. Here is the weird thing: the harder you try to be perfect—try to ignore the shadow and pretend it's not there—the larger your shadow grows!

Jung believed that not only individuals but whole nations can have shadows. Trump is America's shadow, the expression of everything that we as a polite society try to repress, try to pretend doesn't exist.

When we try to tell ourselves that we are better than that, that we are perfect people who are better than the things we look down on, we create a problem. What if taking the moral high ground and shaming people for not being morally upright is part of what caused the shadow to gain power in the first place?

There is real misogyny, real racism, in the soul and psyche of some of our fellow Americans. So why am I talking about looking at our own hearts and minds first? Because that is what you have the power to control, and that is what you are responsible for. Change in society radiates outward, from the self to the whole. Trying to change things the other way around, changing your neighbor instead of yourself, quickly creates all sorts of problems.

Show people what is right without shaming them, and they just might join you. The best path forward is inclusive, not divisive; it is about togetherness, not us versus them. According to Jung, everybody has at least a little bit of the shadow in them. The harder a nation tries to suppress its own shadow and pretend that they are too good for it, the stronger that shadow grows.

....

If pride feeds the shadow, humility weakens it.

....

Trump is all of the pent-up and repressed energies of the American psyche spewed forth. Trump is driven by fear and jealousy, driven to destroy all the best impulses of our democracy—to tear down our natural impulse toward helping others, toward humility, diplomacy, inclusion, tolerance, and grace. Trump is the nation's shadow let loose to rampage and cause destruction. Jealousy, ignorance, pride, and selfishness given free rein to attack all that it does not understand.

Facing one's shadow is not easy. Jung said, "People will do anything, no matter how absurd, to avoid facing their own souls." Facing our shadow is one of the very hardest things a person or a nation can do. It's unpleasant. Many liberals are not going to like my reasoning here. Because it is so much easier to say—What! The foul shadow creature, it is not my fault, it has nothing to do with me! I am not racist, I am not a misogynist, I am not greedy for money, etc.! I am so much better than that!

The only way to handle one's shadow is by integrating it; in Jungian terms, that is what lessens its power. That means recognizing the part of the shadow that is within ourselves. When we do that, we are a lot less likely to repress the shadow and give it strength. We must find a way to speak to those we disagree with, without anger and judgment, in order to shine light into the darkness of ignorance.

The battle is in the heart. The thing that defeats the shadow is light. Shadows grow in secret; denying they exist only makes them stronger. Acknowledge the good and the bad, in yourself and in the psyche of the nation, in everyone. It is balance that steals a shadow's power.

Pope Francis by Christian DeFilippo

32.

DO NOT BUILD WALLS

Love recognizes no barriers. It jumps hurdles, leaps fences, penetrates
walls to arrive at its destination full of hope.
—Maya Angelou

ACTION
Build bridges not walls.

RESULT
Freedom and liberty for all.

It's fine if you agree with me sometimes, and other times not. That's great, in fact. You should only worry when you find yourself in a group of people that all think completely alike. Our strength is that we have a lot of different ideas and viewpoints, and maybe we don't agree 100 percent on every detail. We have many different reasons why we are drawn together and united in our stand against this administration, and that is good.

We should embrace that diversity and not build walls among ourselves. Always strive for unity as the highest guiding principle. What I mean by that is, if someone is against Trump, they are on the same side as us. That goes for Democrats and anarchists, that goes for conservatives and liberals, that goes for Christians, Buddhists, Muslims, Jews, atheists, everyone.

There is a tendency among humans to group people into different categories. When people feel threatened, when they feel afraid, they are much more likely to give up their own freedom and power and turn to someone who they perceive as being "strong" to take control, to be in charge. This often comes with the herd mentality, the desire to belong to an "in-group." The cost of being a part of that in-group is creating an outsider, a scapegoat, a group of people to blame. It's simplistic, and it's an old story, a feature of human nature, a relic of tribalism.

It is obviously incredibly important that we do not fall prey to this terrible flaw of the human mind. I see people on the left doing it all the time, sadly. Progressives who judge others for not being progressive enough. There is always someone with more radical politics, more liberal views about capitalism, or gender views, or race politics, or whatever, and then progressives get divided up into different camps and ideologies. It is not time to divide, it is time to flow together. The future of this planet may very well hinge on the question of whether we can learn to stop putting people in boxes, stop building walls of separation. The side that can be the most inclusive, inviting, welcoming, and open will decide the future, it's simple math.

....

America's strength is in its diversity.

....

33.
HAVE COURAGE

*The ultimate measure of a man is not where he stands in
moments of comfort and convenience, but where he stands at
times of challenge and controversy.*
—Martin Luther King Jr.

ACTION
Take courage!

RESULT
Optimism and confidence
translate into action.

Let's talk about courage. At the end of the day, I think that it matters more than just about anything else. It takes courage to fight for your beliefs. It takes courage to stand up for what you know is right, and to raise your voice.

The opposite of courage is cowardice. It is by cowardice that Trump raised his banner; he operates by milking cowardice, by feeding fears. He made people afraid that Mexican immigrants were going to take their jobs, and that Muslim immigrants were going to be radical terrorists. The antidote for fear is courage.

Malcolm X by Anne Pomel

Not only in individuals, but in nations; and there is a battle between fear and courage happening.

Donald Trump did an excellent job of finding out the fears of his base and magnifying them.

I believe courage and truth ultimately will always conquer fear and darkness. When we look at the past few centuries, we see greater and greater movement toward liberation, toward freedom and equality. Compare our society right now to where we were when America started in 1776; as you know, women couldn't vote, blacks were slaves, and as a nation we were in the midst of committing genocide against most of the native population of North America.

We really have come a long way from where we were a few hundred years ago. So, take heart. We can and we must go much further still. When you look at the big picture of history, the Trump era is part of an ongoing struggle, the march toward a more fair and just society, and that march has always been fueled by courage. People had to fight for their rights. It took courage every step of the way. Slavery was abolished in 1865, but then a whole century passed before the civil rights movement of the 1960s. Change takes persistent commitment and courage.

It took guts to march with Martin Luther King Jr., you better believe it! Using nonviolent civil disobedience, the protestors of the civil rights era forced America to deal with the issues of segregation and racism that had been accepted as the legal status quo. Were it not for the individual acts of courage of every person involved, from Rosa Parks to those who marched from Selma to Montgomery, Alabama, despite tear gas, despite being beaten by police with clubs, despite the fact that some people were killed by angry mobs, they protested in the face of armed troopers and municipal governments that wanted them just to shut up and accept things as they were.

If it weren't for the courage of those who fought for what they knew was right, our society would not have changed. A society that is unjust and unfair will stay frozen in the status quo until enough people, with enough courage, work hard enough to move the dial, to change the balance.

There is work to be done, and it is going to require more from us than just being e-mail activists, Facebook rebels, and Twitter protestors. When we talk about the Resistance, we need to be talking about real life. When we look to the movements of the past, we see real-life rebels, and real-life courage. The outcome of where we go from here will be decided by the courage we bring to the resistance today.

Courage is contagious.

34.
VOTE

Big corporations have money and power to make sure every rule breaks their way; people have voices and votes to push back.
—Elizabeth Warren

ACTION
Vote!

RESULT
Win!

L et's not forget the obvious here, at the end of the day we still have the vote to get Trump out of office. The 2016 presidential election was the fourth time in history that the Electoral College has awarded the presidency to a candidate who actually lost the popular vote, but Trump was by far the biggest loser to still get elected.

We don't have to wait until Election Day 2020 to vote against Trump. The American people can express their disapproval with Trump by voting in local elections.

Make it costly to bargain with Trump, so that politicians who work with him and his morally bankrupt administration know they do so at their own peril. This means voting out politicians that work with Trump, and rewarding politicians that stand up to this administration. This is how to steer democracy. Vote and help to get the vote out. It would be silly to do all of the other resistance activities and forget the power of the vote.

Midterm elections matter. The vote in 2018 will set the stage for what happens in 2020! If voters make it apparent to senators and Congress that supporting Trump's agenda is fatal to their careers, they will abandon Trump's agenda. Demand exactly what you want from your local politicians, and vote accordingly.

Stay involved on a local level. It isn't just about Trump, we have to take back the country from the grass roots on up, city council member by city council member, US senator by US senator, election by election. Think of voting as just the first and most basic step, and consider helping to get out the vote by phone banking and canvassing.

35.

EMBRACE YOUR INNER RADICAL

Radical simply means grasping things at the root.
—Angela Davis

ACTION
Don't be afraid to think like a radical.

RESULT
Radical change.

What does it mean to be radical? At one point in history it was considered radical to imagine a world without kings and queens as rulers. It was once radical to imagine an America that did not belong to Great Britain as a colony. It was once radical to imagine a world without slavery. It was once radical to imagine a world where women had the right to vote.

The people who first fought for those ideals were called crazy and dreamers and radicals. They were put in jail. They persisted. They took action. They did much more than engage in whatever in those years was akin to "Internet activism." They took it to the streets and fought for the causes they believed in, in real life. Would they have used the Internet as a tool if it had been around? Absolutely. Use the Internet, but don't stop there.

Radical means giving a damn about the things that are important to you. It means treating things that actually matter like they actually matter. It is living compassionately and purposefully. These values should not really even be called "radical," which implies unusual. The day that being informed and caring about the choices we make as a people and as a nation, the day that kind of compassion and action is normal, instead of unusual, is the day that we will undergo a profound and real transformation.

Democratic Socialists of America

Just as earlier in the book I may have gone out of some readers' comfort zones when I asked you to consider prayer and meditation as tools in the battle of the resistance, if this section feels like a stretch, then it was written for you. I'd like to broach the *S* word. Socialism. I think we all agree that what is needed is fresh ideas and policies that are beneficial to everyday people. We can't let Trump, the plutocracy, and henchmen like Paul Ryan and Mitch McConnell win this fight. As I've said before, though, it is not enough to stand against something; we need to stand for something, and stand for ideas that are bold and beneficial to everybody, not just the rich. I think that's exactly why the candidacy and ideas of Bernie Sanders captured the energy and spirits of so many young people during the primaries—people were ready to acknowledge that these ideas don't sound so "radical" and "crazy," like I've been told. They sound like good common sense.

Which is why I'd like to point to the Democratic Socialists of America as setting a great example of the kinds of things people can push for when they aren't afraid to be called radical. Look at Bernie!

Life is short, and democracy is fragile, freedom is hard fought for—should we not strive to be the best country that we can imagine becoming? What better place to start than valuing the citizen over the corporation? The message of economic equality for all is one that people can get excited about in every state, red or blue, when the essence of the message is fully understood. Since Trump was elected, there has been a big upswing of people getting involved in the Democratic Socialists of America; I believe that is because socialism is a philosophy that cuts to the heart of the matter and defends the interests of the working class. Democratic socialism is not the same thing as Marxism or communism, but a philosophy within the Democratic Party that believes the country and the economy should be run democratically by and for the people, not just by and for the wealthy few. Also, they believe everybody should have health care!

Wherever you are on the political spectrum, I encourage you to fully explore this and other strategies and philosophies of resistance! I encourage you to explore new avenues for expressing your voice, for finding your part to play in the resistance, wherever that may be.

It Is Time to Chart a New Course!

The core of the Far Right's rabid base are aging old Fox News fans and uneducated white dudes. Are we going to be outmaneuvered by people who can't tell fact from fiction? By people who don't read? Hell no! We got this! If we don't let ourselves be divided by petty bickering, if we stand together, united by the common causes of equality and fairness for all, we will be unbeatable.

Being a radical means waking up to the fact that the fight for a just society, the fight that includes America's greatest heroes, from Woody Guthrie to Malcolm X, from Susan B. Anthony to Cesar Chavez, is (and always has been) happening NOW. Happening here, and happening now, and happening because of people like you. To be radical is to be a participant, to be radical is to be someone who is consciously shaping history by choice.

It means using the same tactics and techniques that radicals have always used, to fight and to win, and the Resistance has been around forever. Protest music, pamphlets, strikes, boycotts, organizing, marching, singing and chanting in the streets, civil unrest, civil disobedience, taking to the airwaves, the Internet, using Facebook to spread the message, using any form of media available. Being radical here, now, at this point in time, is about embracing the rich history of protest from the Boston Tea Party to Black Lives Matter and #MeToo, and moving it forward, keeping it alive and growing.

The future is at stake and the time is now.

36.
CREATE THE FUTURE

We have to assume that we are responsible for the future of this world.
—James Baldwin

ACTION
Decide what happens next.

RESULT
That's up to you.

You are here, where you are in life, as a result of every choice that you have made. You have been shaped by your beliefs, by the company you keep, your friends and family, and to some extent by random stuff that has happened to you, but I believe we happen to life more than life happens to us. Not everybody believes that, but that's how it is. Little by little, day by day, we create ourselves, often through habit and repetitions, but also, sometimes, consciously, willfully, and by choice.

A nation is the same way, except that it is a huge collection of people, so sure, it's a lot more complicated, but basically "We the People" is every American that lives in this big place, from sea to shining sea, from purple mountains to amber waves of

Abbie Hoffman by Luke Ramsey

grain, the whole enchilada—we the folks living here right now are responsible for what happens next. That is what a democracy is. That is all that it is. We can make this place anything, anything at all that we want it to be!

There have always been people who try to subvert democracy to serve themselves. There will always be people who seek to subvert our freedoms for their own selfish gains. It's an age-old story, as old as the first democracy.

The struggle is nothing new. Greed for wealth and lust for power were not invented by Trump. The struggle within this democracy between the rich and corrupt and everybody else is as old as America, it is the struggle of history.

What Happens Next?

Perhaps this struggle against the malignant cancer in our government is the birthing pains of something even bigger. What happens if we resist this demagogue, and when he is defeated, we don't stop? What could we achieve then? What happens if we take the energy that is fomenting right now against tyranny, against ignorance and lies, and against the corporate plutocracy and we keep pushing? What happens if we don't stop after Trump has been defeated? What if we keep using all the tactics of resistance, using the strengthened energy, and networks, and awareness, and motivation, and we just keep going? Where can we get to from here? Imagine what that could look like!

The final action of this book is to envision the version of

America you want to see materialize. What is the version of our future that is worth fighting for? Take a moment and write down a description of what you want us to become. Think of it as planting a seed.

The shape of the future will be determined by you and people like you, those who dare to resist. History has shown that when We the People wake up, when we get involved, when we organize, when we act with courage, it is possible to survive, to fight, and to liberate ourselves from tyranny. When freedom, equality, and the truth are at stake, those who take action, brave men and women like yourself, have the power to boldly shape the future.